Treasures

INTERACTIVE
Read-Aloud
ANTHOLOGY with PLAYS

Grade 6

**Macmillan
McGraw-Hill**

ACKNOWLEDGMENTS

"Dangerous Rescues Are Part of Job for Coast Guard" by Zoltan Istvan from *National Geographic News*. Copyright © 2004 by National Geographic. Used by permission of National Geographic.

Excerpt from THE SEARCH FOR LOST CITIES by Nicola Barber. Copyright © 1998 by Steck-Vaughn Company. Used by permission of Raintree Steck-Vaughn Publishers, an imprint of Steck-Vaughn Company.

"Becky Schroeder: Enlightened Thinker" from BRAINSTORM!: THE STORIES OF TWENTY AMERICAN KID INVENTORS by Tom Tucker. Copyright © 1995 by Tom Tucker. Used by permission of Farrar, Straus and Giroux.

"Remember the Bridge" from REMEMBER THE BRIDGE: POEMS OF A PEOPLE by Carole Boston Weatherford. Copyright © 2002 by Carole Boston Weatherford. Used by permission of Philomel Books, a division of Penguin Putnam Books for Young Readers.

"Bringing Back Salmon" by Jeffrey Rich from *Ranger Rick*, October 2003. Copyright © 2003 by the National Wildlife Foundation. Used by permission of the National Wildlife Foundation.

"Shortstop" from KNOTS IN MY YO-YO STRING: THE AUTOBIOGRAPHY OF A KID by Jerry Spinelli. Copyright © 1998 by Jerry Spinelli. Used by permission of Alfred A. Knopf, Inc.

"How Fisher Went to the Skyland: The Origin of the Big Dipper" from KEEPERS OF THE EARTH: NATIVE AMERICAN STORIES AND ENVIRONMENTAL ACTIVITIES FOR CHILDREN by Michael J. Caduto and Joseph Bruchac. Copyright © 1988, 1989 by Michael J. Caduto and Joseph Bruchac. Used by permission of the author of this story, Joseph Bruchac.

"Helping Hands" from *Current Health*, February 2003. Copyright © 2003 by Weekly Reader Corporation. Used by permission of Weekly Reader Corporation.

"The Magical Horse" from TONGUES OF JADE by Laurence Yep. Copyright © 1991 by Laurence Yep. Used by permission of HarperCollins Publishers.

Excerpt from SLED DOGS: ARCTIC ATHLETES by Elizabeth Ring. Copyright © 1994 by Elizabeth Ring. Used by permission of The Millbrook Press.

"Pecos Bill Invents the Lariat" was originally entitled "Pecos Bill Invents Modern Cowpunching" in PECOS BILL, THE GREATEST COWBOY OF ALL TIMES by James Cloyd Bowman. Copyright © 1937, 1964 by Albert Whitman & Company. All rights reserved. Used by permission of Albert Whitman & Company.

"Notes on the Art of Poetry" by Dylan Thomas. Used by permission.

"I Made a Perpetual Motion Machine" from A PIZZA THE SIZE OF THE SUN by Jack Prelutsky. Copyright © 1996 by Jack Prelutsky. Used by permission of Greenwillow/William Morrow.

DIG THIS!: HOW ARCHEOLOGISTS UNCOVER OUR PAST by Michael Avi-Yonah. Copyright © 1993 by Runestone Press. Used by permission of Runestone Press/Lerner Publications Company.

"Letter to the Media" by students of DeWitt Middle School. Copyright © 2005 by PBS. Used by permission of PBS.

"No Barriers" from A SPECIAL STRENGTH by Michael Burgan. Copyright © The McGraw-Hill Companies, Inc.

Continued on page 260

B

The **McGraw·Hill** Companies

Mc Graw Hill **Macmillan McGraw-Hill**

Published by Macmillan/McGraw-Hill, of McGraw-Hill Education, a division of The McGraw-Hill Companies, Inc., Two Penn Plaza, New York, New York 10121.

Printed in the United States of America

3 4 5 6 7 8 9 10 079 11 10 09 08 07 06

CONTENTS

Unit 6

Plays

INTERACTIVE
Read-Aloud
ANTHOLOGY with PLAYS

Developing Listening Comprehension

Read Alouds help to build students' listening comprehension. This anthology offers selections from a variety of genres, including biography, fiction, folk tales, nonfiction, primary sources, songs, and poetry, to share with students. Instruction is provided with each selection to develop specific **comprehension strategies.** Students are asked to **set a purpose for listening,** as well as to **determine the author's purpose** for writing. Using the instruction provided, each Read Aloud becomes an enjoyable, purposeful learning experience.

What Makes a Read Aloud Interactive?

With each selection, **Teacher Think Alouds** are provided to help you model the use of comprehension strategies during reading. Using Think Alouds allows students to listen and to observe how a good reader uses strategies to get meaning from text. After reading, students are given the opportunity to apply the comprehension strategy. Students are asked to Think Aloud as they apply the strategy. By listening to a **Student Think Aloud** you can determine if the student is applying the comprehension strategy appropriately and with understanding.

Think-Aloud Copying Masters included in the Read-Aloud Anthology provide sentence starters to help students Think Aloud about a strategy.

PLAYS

Reader's Theater for Building Fluency

You can use the plays and choral readings found at the back of this anthology to perform a Reader's Theater with students. Reading fluency is developed by repeated practice in reading text, especially when the reading is done orally. Reader's Theater can help build students' fluency skills because it engages them in a highly motivating activity that provides an opportunity to read—and reread—text orally. As students practice their assigned sections of the "script," they have multiple opportunities to increase their accuracy in word recognition and their rate of reading. Students are also strongly motivated to practice reading with appropriate phrasing and expression.

Performing Reader's Theater

• Assign speaking roles.

• Do not always assign the speaking role with the most text to the most fluent reader. Readers who need practice reading need ample opportunity to read.

• Have students rehearse by reading and rereading their lines over several days. In these rehearsals, allow time for teacher and peer feedback about pace, phrasing, and expression.

• Students do not memorize their lines, but rather read their lines from the script.

• No sets, costumes, or props are necessary.

Dangerous Rescues Are Part of Job for Coast Guard

by Zoltan Istvan

Genre: Informational Nonfiction

Comprehension Strategy: Analyze Story Structure

Think-Aloud Copying Master number 2

Before Reading

Genre: Inform students that you will read aloud a nonfiction article that recounts the event of a Coast Guard rescue. The article also points out the purpose of the Coast Guard and the risks that guards face.

Expand Vocabulary: To help students understand critical details in the selection, explain the following words:

> *diabetic:* caused by diabetes, a medical disorder
>
> *coordinates:* sets of numbers that describe the exact locations of places
>
> *chaotic:* out of control
>
> *treacherous:* filled with hidden dangers

Set a Purpose for Reading: Invite students to listen to this selection to find out why bravery is an important trait for Coast Guard members.

During Reading

Use the Think Alouds during the first reading of the story. Notes about the genre may be used during subsequent readings.

Dangerous Rescues Are Part of Job for Coast Guard

by Zoltan Istvan

Sailor Mitch Powell, en route from San Diego, went into diabetic shock 18 miles (29 kilometers) off the coast of Oregon an hour before sundown. Stranded aboard his crippled 30-foot (9-meter) yacht *Sway,* his last words to the Chetco River Station Coast Guard in Harbor, Oregon, were: "I can't feel my legs. I'm going into shock."

The rescue effort, aggravated by 15-foot (4.5-meter) seas, chilling winds at 35 knots, and the fading rays of daylight, was going to be one of the most challenging that year.[1]

The Chetco River Station, where the average age of the nearly 50 guardsmen is just 25 years old, is a breeding ground for tough work and hair-raising rescues. Established in 1961, Chetco is just one of dozens of Coast Guard stations along the Pacific Northwest—an area extending from northern California to the tip of Alaska. Every year some of the most radical rescue operations in the world take place along the Oregon, Washington, and Alaskan coastlines.

"There's no question about it. We have some of the most difficult weather and rough seas anywhere on the planet," said 44-year-old Master Chief Boatswain James Bankson, the 25-year Coast Guard veteran in charge of the Chetco River Station. "Add freezing water, fog, and darkness to a rescue, like the *Sway,* and it becomes a very dangerous situation for everyone involved."

Wild Rescue

As night fell, the circumstances of the vessel Sway and its captain worsened. Rising seas and darkness took their toll. Unable to board the Sway due to violence of the waves and the yacht's broken mast swinging about wildly, Chetco's primary vessel, a 47-foot (14-meter), million-dollar, aluminum motorboat known as number 47237, was forced to motor at a 22-yard (20-meter) radius around the flailing yacht. Medical attention to Powell would have to wait until a safer approach was determined.

Boat *47237* was soon joined by an identical boat from Oregon's Rogue River Detachment Coast Guard unit, 35 miles (56 kilometers) away from *Sway's* coordinates. A 23-foot (7-meter)

Think Aloud

[1] As I read about the dangers people face on the water and what the Coast Guard does to help, I can see a pattern of problem and solution. The author lays out several problems at once—a man going into shock in a damaged boat during a storm! So what's the solution? Oh, I see, a rescue effort by the Coast Guard.

utility boat and a Coast Guard HH-65A Dolphin helicopter, used primarily to illuminate the <u>chaotic</u> scene with its powerful overhead spotlight, also joined the rescue. Divers were never allowed to swim to the *Sway* because they might be lost in the darkness or crack their skulls on the hull of the rocking sailboat.

In the end, the utility boat, captained by Bankson, was able to pull up along *Sway* for an instant and allow Coast Guard serviceman Tom Wunder and medic Chris Dodson to jump aboard without getting into the water or being hit by the swinging mast.

"It was my first rescue that involved a helicopter," said Crystal Castle, a 20-year-old 3rd Class Boatswain Mate from the Chetco River Station. "A helicopter really makes a rescue that is much more dynamic and intense—especially in the dark when the noise of the helicopter, ocean, and boat engines are roaring, and the spotlights are flashing everywhere."[2]

Treacherous Waters, Many Rescues

A rescue of this magnitude is not uncommon along this stretch of coast. The Chetco River Station alone accomplished 225 search and rescue missions in 2003, saving 27 lives, said Bankson.

Many of the most dangerous rescues involved commercial fishermen, whose wooden or rusty boats are not always up to par. Commercial fishing for crab, salmon, and tuna along the Pacific Northwest thrives and fishermen number in the thousands.[3]

"I've been involved in a couple incidents where the Coast Guard helped save boats and crew," said John Fraser, a commercial fisherman based in Harbor, Oregon, and captain of the 41-foot (12.5-meter) wooden boat *Njord*. "The weather can be tough in this area and change at a moment's notice. It's nice to have the Coast Guard standing by a radio 24 hours a day, listening for any distress calls."

The Pacific Northwest Coast Guard, like all other Coast Guard groups in America, is a branch of the armed services; during peacetime the Coast Guard operates as part of the Department of Homeland Security, and during wartime it falls under direction of the Navy. Coast Guards were used in the war efforts in Iraq, and all recruits, whether in wartime or not, are trained to use firearms.

Think Aloud

[2] I can see why the author includes this quote from one of the guards. She describes the rescue scene really well. I think this is important because it helps me picture just how exciting and dangerous the job really is.

Think Aloud

[3] I can make a connection when I read about commercial fishermen. I once watched a news program that traced the fish we buy from the ocean to the market. Workers on a commercial fishing trip may spend long hours or even days at sea, hauling in heavy nets loaded with fish. But now I realize that bad weather can make their job dangerous.

Nonfiction Article:
Accurate details are
an important part of
a nonfiction article.
When reporting an
actual event, the writer
has to make sure every
single detail is correct.
So Zoltan Istvan
doesn't just say if a
boat is big or small,
he gives the exact
measurements in feet
and meters.

With about 40,000 personnel, the Coast Guard has recently taken on a greater role in national security after September 11, 2001. The United States government is utilizing the guardsmen to more closely patrol and protect its coastlines from possible terrorist attacks and intrusions.

National Defense

"Mostly what we do is rescues," said Lieutenant Commander Thomas Durand, of the group Airstation Surface Operation in North Bend, Oregon. "But our other duties depend on a wide range of factors and can involve keeping foreign fishermen out of our waters and searching boats for terrorists' weapons."

They are also charged with responding to hazardous chemical spills, educating people in boating safety, and intercepting illegal immigrants at sea.

At the Chetco River Station, Bankson recommended six Coast Guard achievement medals be awarded to his staff for their efforts in saving Mitch Powell. Just after one o'clock in the morning, *Sway* was towed into Brookings Harbor, Oregon, where Powell was taken to a hospital and eventually made a full recovery.

"Sometimes this job can be scary and life threatening. But that's the nature of the job and we have to do it," said Castle. "It's a great feeling to rescue people and know you really helped someone."

After Reading

Summarize: Reread the selection for students. Ask them to summarize each time you finish reading a section.

Student Think Aloud

Use Copying Master number 2 to prompt students as they connect information they have read in the article to what they have learned in the past.

"I made a connection when . . ."

Think and Respond

1. Why might someone want to be a part of the Coast Guard? *Possible responses: A person might like the idea of helping other people in trouble; a person might enjoy boats and the excitement and danger of the ocean; a person might like helping our country by patrolling our coasts.* **Critical**

2. What are some problems the Coast Guard solves? *Possible responses: rescuing stranded sailors; protecting coastlines from terrorist attacks; searching boats for weapons; responding to hazardous chemical spills; educating people in boating safety; intercepting illegal immigrants at sea.* **Genre**

3. Why do you think Zoltan Istvan wrote about the Coast Guard? *Possible responses: Perhaps he has been involved with the Coast Guard or has been rescued by its members; he wants others to understand the difficult work the Coast Guard does.* **Author's Purpose**

The Search for Lost Cities
by Nicola Barber

Genre: Informational Nonfiction

Comprehension Strategy: Analyze Text Structure

Think-Aloud Copying Master number 4

Before Reading

Genre: Tell students that you will be reading aloud a nonfiction selection about lost cities, once thriving places that for one reason or another no longer exist. Explain that the purpose of informational nonfiction is to inform the reader about the topic.

Expand Vocabulary: To help students understand the work of archaeologists, introduce the following words:

decline: a gradual ending of something

evidence: signs of the existence or truth of something

archaeologists: scientists who study materials left by ancient cultures

inhabited: lived in, especially by human beings

Set a Purpose for Reading: Suggest that students listen carefully to the article to answer the opening question of the selection: "How do cities get lost?"

During Reading

Use the Think Alouds during the first reading of the story. Notes about the genre and cultural perspectives may be used during subsequent readings.

The Search for Lost Cities

by Nicola Barber

How do cities get lost?

It's hard to imagine today's modern cities being abandoned and becoming "lost." How could anyone forget a city as large and as famous as New York, or Paris, or London?[1] The answer, of course, is that cities do not usually just disappear overnight. Often, they <u>decline</u> over many years, until the last people leave their homes, and the buildings fall into ruins. Some abandoned cities are gradually covered by dust and mud until they are nothing but shapeless mounds. Some are swallowed by jungle, and their once grand buildings are smothered and hidden by plants. Others are pulled down as people remove building materials to construct their own new settlements nearby. Gradually, people forget that there was ever a bustling city in their area, and as the memory fades the city is "lost."

How does a city die?

There are many possible reasons for the death of a city. For example, some cities grew up beside busy trade routes. But sometimes trade decreased, and then the city declined, too. In other places, changes in the climate affected the life of cities. Perhaps the land around a city became less fertile, so there was not enough food to feed all its inhabitants, and gradually people had to move away.

The end of other cities was more sudden and spectacular. Natural disasters such as earthquakes and volcanic eruptions wiped out places, such as Pompeii. Sometimes, fires burned down whole cities. And sometimes, cities were destroyed on purpose. The magnificent city of Persepolis, the capital of the Persian Empire in the 6th century BC, was burned down by the army of Alexander the Great in 330 BC.

Finding lost cities

Although cities may be abandoned for many years, they are not usually truly lost. Often, the local people will know of hidden ruins or mysterious buried walls. It is only when an outsider comes looking for <u>evidence</u> of a forgotten city that

---

Think Aloud

[1] *I figured out that cause and effect will be important in this selection because right away the author asks* how *and* why *questions. Lost cities are the* effect, *but what causes them? The author says there are* many *reasons, or causes. For example, when trade slowed down, it caused cities near trade routes to decline. I keep seeing other signal words for cause and effect as well. The word* so *is a short way of saying* as a result. *The word* affected *tells me that changes in the weather caused some cities to change, too.*

anyone realizes what the ruins really are. This was true of Hiram Bingham, who was led to the Inca ruins of Machu Picchu by a local man who knew exactly where they were. In other places, archaeologists have painstakingly put together evidence to work out what a city was once like.

Unsolved mysteries

Today, excavating lost towns and cities is the work of highly trained teams of archaeologists. The days of amateur treasure hunters searching ruins for gold and other valuable objects are gone. But amazing finds are being made and new sites are still being uncovered, which all add to our knowledge of the past. Often, a new discovery forces archaeologists and historians to change their ideas about the past. Sometimes something so strange and unusual is found that it creates a whole new mystery. . . .

A theory disproved

When a Greek archaeologist, Spyridon Marinatos, began excavations on the island of Thera (Santorini) in 1967, he was hoping to find out the truth about the end of the Minoan civilization. The Minoans lived on Crete, about 62 miles (100 km) south of Thera, until around 1500 bc, when some sort of disaster brought their civilization to an end. Professor Marinatos thought the cause may have been a huge volcanic eruption on Thera that would have sent out clouds of dust and ash and set off huge tidal waves.

Professor Marinatos decided to excavate on Thera itself to find out more about the eruption. He dug deep trenches around the village of Akrotiri in the south of the island. Here he found houses preserved under the ash, just like those at Pompeii. But he found no human skeletons. It seems that the people had time to escape before the worst of the eruption.[2] By working out the age of pieces of pottery and other remains, Professor Marinatos decided that Akrotiri had been abandoned some years before the destruction of Knossos on Crete. This means that the eruption happened before the end of the Minoan civilization. So the destruction of Knossos is still a mystery to be solved some time in the future.

Think Aloud

[2] I notice the author shows how one action is linked to another, and that what happens as a result isn't always what I expect. For example, the author tells me why Professor Marinatos excavated the island of Thera. He wanted to find out why the Minoan civilization ended. He thought it had been caused by an eruption that killed the inhabitants, but he was wrong. The author explains that not finding skeletons still had an effect—it disproved the professor's theory.

History beneath the surface

In many modern towns and cities, history lies not very far beneath the surface! Many towns and cities are built on sites that have been inhabited for centuries. Obviously, archaeologists can't excavate easily where there are modern stores, offices, or houses. But if a building is pulled down to make space for redevelopment, it is sometimes possible for the archaeologists to excavate the site first.

This is what has been happening in the city of York, in England. Archaeologists have gradually uncovered a Viking city, called Jorvik, beneath the modern city. Underneath the city center, they have discovered the business center of Jorvik, where craftspeople, such as jewelers and woodworkers, made and sold their goods. From their finds, they have been able to determine what life in the Viking city may have been like.

Legendary cities

There are some "lost" cities that will probably never be found. These are the cities that are described in legends, folk tales, and myths. The descriptions may once have been based on real places, but today we do not know where the cities were or even whether they ever really existed. Camelot, the legendary court and capital of King Arthur, is one of these places. Many people think that Cadbury Castle in Somerset, England, is the site of Camelot. Others say that the tale of King Arthur is just a story, and that Camelot was not a real place.

The strange tale of Atlantis is a mixture of history and legend.[3] The Greek philosopher Plato (427–347 BC) wrote about the mysterious story of Atlantis, which is not a lost city but a whole lost island! The island is supposed to have disappeared under the waves after a volcanic eruption. Many people have tried to prove that the tale of Atlantis is actually the story of the end of the Minoan civilization. Others have suggested that Atlantis lies deep below the waves of the Atlantic Ocean. It is just one of the many mysteries of ancient times that may never be solved.

Think Aloud

[3] *I think learning about legendary cities is important because not all lost cities may be found. Some cities, such as Camelot and Atlantis, may never have existed except in legends and myths. Many people believe they were real places, but so far no evidence has been found for either place.*

After Reading

Take Notes: Reread the selection for students. Ask them to take notes on any information that helps them understand how cities become "lost."

Student Think Aloud

Use Copying Master number 4 to prompt students to explain how the author includes information that shows how cities become lost.

"I figured out _____ because . . ."

Think and Respond

1. What are some of the reasons cities become lost? *Possible responses: decreased trade; climate changes; loss of resources; natural disasters; destruction in war* **Analytical**

2. Why does the author use subheadings? *Possible responses: Subheadings help the reader quickly see what the selection is about; they make it easier to find specific information; they make lengthy text easier to read.* **Genre**

3. The author says that some lost cities were as large and famous as cities of today. Why do you think she wrote this selection? *Possible responses: She wants to explain that lost cities were not tiny places with few people; she wants to show that today's cities could someday be lost, too.* **Author's Purpose**

Becky Schroeder, Enlightened Thinker

Genre: Nonfiction

Comprehension Strategy: Make Inferences and Analyze

Think-Aloud Copying Master number 6

Before Reading

Genre: Announce that you will be reading aloud a nonfiction selection about a young inventor who wanted to solve an everyday problem. Encourage students to recall other nonfiction they may have read about inventors.

Expand Vocabulary: Before reading the selection, share definitions of the following words:

> *inspirations:* things that lead to creative thought or action
>
> *exposure:* contact with something or someone
>
> *potential:* possible
>
> *distributor:* company that helps sell large numbers of products to stores

Set a Purpose for Reading: Ask students to listen to the selection to find out what problem Becky decided to solve and determine if she succeeded.

During Reading

Use the Think Alouds during the first reading of the story. Notes about the genre may be used during subsequent readings.

Becky Schroeder, Enlightened Thinker

by Tom Tucker

Rebecca Schroeder entered the world of invention at the age of ten, while a pupil at Ladyfield Academy in Toledo, Ohio. One October evening, she had gone with her mother to a shopping center and was waiting in the car, poring over her studies, while her mother hurried in for some groceries.

"I was in the car doing my homework when it started to get dark," she told reporters later. "I kept thinking what a good thing it would be if people could write in the dark."[1]

Her father encouraged her to pursue her inspirations. "I'm always coming up with ideas," explained Becky when the media thronged around her. "It happens when you least expect it."

At first, she kept the idea to herself. The homework arrived on the teacher's desk the next day, but the idea of writing in the dark glimmered in her mind for many days, until she went to the library to find out what kinds of things glow in the dark.

"Fluorescence" was the word she had in mind. Wrong— fluorescent compounds fade just after they're removed from the light. Next she considered "bioluminescence," meaning the emission of light by organisms. Glowworms? Fireflies? Would some living creature light her inspiration? When that didn't seem promising, Becky discovered "phosphorescence," the action of certain substances that produce a glow after exposure to light.

At first, she thought of an ink that would glow in the dark, but then she had another idea: what about coating the surface of something like a clipboard with phosphorescent material? Then, if she set writing paper on top, the board would glow through, silhouetting any letters on the paper, thereby making them visible in the dark.[2]

Charles Schroeder describes it this way: "She came home. She said, 'I have an invention.' I said, 'Oh.' Then her mother said, 'I think she really does.' "

The next step? A trip to a hobby shop to get phosphorescent paint. Then she needed a room with no windows, so she commandeered

Think Aloud

[1] I am able to picture in my mind just what problem Becky had. I can just imagine being in the car, trying to write on a piece of paper. As the sun sets, the light gets dimmer until I cannot see well. I can understand Becky's problem and why she wanted to fix it.

Think Aloud

[2] At first I thought this might be a story about someone who invents something because he or she wants to make a lot of money. I found out that was not the case for Becky. She wants her invention to solve a problem. I'll keep reading to see if she also wants to make a lot of money.

one of the family's bathrooms for her laboratory. And one evening, after her first experiments, Becky Schroeder ran into the family room, shouting, "Come see! It works!"

Charles Schroeder was impressed. "The thing worked better than I thought it could have worked," he says. In the blackness, his daughter held up a glowing rectangle on which he could read her message: "I can write in the dark."

Two years later, on August 27, 1974, the U.S. Patent and Trademark Office awarded Becky patent #3,832,556 for a "Luminescent Backing Sheet for Writing in the Dark." Newspapers and magazines rushed to tell her story; she appeared on a number of television shows and won several awards.

In the years that followed, Becky has been granted almost a dozen patents that stake out improvements on her basic idea. Becky formed a company called BJ Products (BJ stands for Becky Jane), and now she calls her product Glo-Sheet.

Who are the <u>potential</u> customers for Glo-Sheet? At various times, both the U.S. Navy and NASA have taken a serious look at the invention. Becky sees many uses for it, for people such as pilots in darkened cockpits; policemen filling out forms and soldiers in war zones at night; doctors, nurses, and other medical personnel making their evening rounds; and movie and theater critics who need to jot notes during shows. But to date, although many Glo-Sheets have been sold directly, Becky has found no <u>distributor</u>.

For her brainstorm, Becky was named an Ohio Inventor of the Year, and was inducted into the Ohio Inventors Hall of Fame. Today, more than twenty years later, she is in demand to speak about invention at state and national meetings, and at schools and universities. Now married, she assists her husband in running his own insurance agency, and she also uses her creativity in designing jewelry for a local store.

To kids, her message is: "Childhood? That's where you start inventing." And she warns them against listening to naysayers, those people, sometimes friends or family, who may unconsciously discourage kid inventors because they themselves do not believe.[3] Becky says, "Keep an open mind—things could come up."

Today, when people hear about Glo-Sheet, they are still intrigued. Kids get excited about writing letters at summer camp after lights-out, for example—or other everyday applications. And they like Becky's story, too, the story of a little girl who conquered the dark with a bright idea.

Think Aloud

[3] *I thought Becky's message to kids was important because children are often more creative than adults. Her message encourages other kids to use their imaginations to think of new ideas and inventions. She warns kids that not everyone will think their ideas have value, but that does not mean the inventors should be discouraged.*

Summarize: Ask students to summarize the selection. Then have students think of an everyday problem and "create" an invention to solve the problem. Have the students draw their invention, label it, and write a short descriptive paragraph about it.

Student Think Aloud

Use Copying Master number 6 to prompt students to discuss Becky's experience and the process of invention.

"I thought _____ was important in this text because . . ."

Think and Respond

1. What does this selection help you understand about inventions in general? *Possible responses: Inventions often come about in order to solve a problem; you don't have to be an adult to come up with a good invention; not all inventions make the inventor rich.* **Critical**

2. The selection begins with Becky trying to do her homework. What stops her? What does she decide to do? What does this tell you about her? *Possible responses: It gets too dark to write; she decides to find a way to write in the dark. She is a creative person.* **Make Inferences and Analyze**

3. What do you think the author wants readers to understand about invention? *Possible responses: Perhaps the author wants to inspire us to invent; he wants to show that ordinary people, and especially kids, can be inventors.* **Author's Purpose**

Remember the Bridge

by Carole Boston Weatherford

Genre: Rhyming Poem

Poetic Element: Repetition

Think-Aloud Copying Master number 1

Before Reading

Genre: Explain that rhyme is only one element of some poems. Poems also use repetition to emphasize a key word or idea. In this poem, the word *remember* is repeated several times. The repetitive pattern of short lines also sets up a rhythm that emphasizes that the message of the poem is an urgent one. The poet is not just encouraging people to remember those who came before, she is also stressing how important it is.

Expand Vocabulary: To help students understand the poem, explain the following words and phrases:

> *ancestors:* relatives from long ago, such as great-great grandparents
>
> *Underground Railroad:* a secret organization that help enslaved workers escape to freedom or safety
>
> *laborers:* workers
>
> *Motherland:* the country in which someone was born

Set a Purpose for Reading: Ask students to listen to the poem to determine what the poet wants people to remember.

During Reading

Use the Think Aloud during the first reading of the poem. Notes about the genre may be used during subsequent readings.

Remember the Bridge

by Carole Boston Weatherford

Think Aloud

I wonder why the poet chose such a dark and heavy image of ancestors crossing a bridge, sweating, and some even losing their lives. Perhaps it is because she wants us to feel the sacrifice these people made. It was not just a journey for them, it was a fight for their lives.

Remember the bridge
    that your <u>ancestors</u> crossed,
    the sweat that was spilled
    and the lives that were lost.

Remember the slaves
    who raised corn and picked cotton.
    Keep singing their songs
    so they won't be forgotten;
    the <u>Underground Railroad</u>
    that passed through at night,
    the signs and conductors
    that guided slaves' flight.

Remember the soldiers
    who fought though they knew
    they might not be free
    when the battle was through.

Remember the old souls
    who handed down tales,
    the bold men and women
    who blazed their own trails
    from the South to the North,
    from farm to big city,
    with satchels of dreams
    and no use for self-pity.

Remember the bootblacks
    who made old shoes shine,
    the industrious <u>laborers</u>
    who manned factory lines.

Remember the housemaids
    who scrubbed dirty floors,
    the leaders who spoke out
    to open closed doors.

Remember the hard way
   the ancestors came:
   snatched from the <u>Motherland</u>
   bound in iron chains.

Remember the voyage,
   the capture, the chase,
   young warriors who vanished
   without even a trace.

Remember the ocean
   much too vast to span,
   long shadows on shorelines
   and footprints in sand.

Forget not the glory
   of Africa's past,
   the temples and riches
   that to this day last:
   bronze, baskets and mud cloth,
   pyramids of stone,
   ebony statues
   and bracelets of bone.

The journey continues,
   the bridge still holds strong,
   hands reach across water,
   hearts sing a new song.

Genre Study

Rhyming Poem:
A poem can say a lot with just a few words. For example, the poet mentions the Underground Railroad but does not explain it in detail. The poet also includes just enough detail to show the kinds of hard labor that enslaved ancestors were forced to do. It makes readers care about the subjects of the poem and be inspired by their courage, without knowing everything about them.

Set a Purpose for Rereading: For subsequent readings, have students listen for phrases that seem especially meaningful or moving. Afterwards, encourage students to discuss these phrases.

Student Think Aloud

Use Copying Master number 1 to prompt students to share a question they have about specific details in the poem.

"I wonder why . . ."

Cultural Perspective

The subjects of the poem had to find their own way to the North. Then they would meet volunteers of the Underground Railroad who would help them find their way to safety. These travelers had to be careful not to be caught, or they could be severely punished and returned to the South as slaves. Have students write a poem about something else in history that should be remembered. Encourage them to use the author's style and emphasis on repetition and rhyme.

Think and Respond

1. How is the use of repetition important in the poem? *Possible responses: It emphasizes the importance of remembering the courage of the ancestors; it gives the poem a powerful rhythm that makes it easier to remember and creates a mood of urgency.* **Critical**

2. Recall an image in the poem that has special meaning for you. Explain why you think it is important. *Responses will vary. Possible response: I liked the image of people carrying satchels of dreams because it reminds me that people did not have much to carry when they left the South to go north. They had only dreams.* **Genre**

3. Why do you think a poet of today wrote a poem about the struggles of people long ago? *Possible response: Perhaps she wanted Americans to always honor the memory of those who risked their lives for freedom.* **Author's Purpose**

Bringing Back Salmon

by Jeffrey Rich

Genre: Informational Nonfiction

Comprehension Strategy: Make Inferences and Analyze

Think-Aloud Copying Master number 1

Before Reading

Genre: Tell students that you are going to read aloud a nonfiction selection about students in California who help bring salmon to a creek where no salmon had swam for 50 years.

Expand Vocabulary: To support students' understanding of the selection, introduce the following words and phrases:

> *polluted:* harmed the environment
>
> *upstream:* toward the source of a river or stream
>
> *fish hatchery:* a place where fish eggs are hatched under artificial conditions
>
> *yolk sacs:* thin membranes surrounding newly hatched fish

Set a Purpose for Reading: Invite students to listen to the selection to find out how the students bring the salmon back to the river.

During Reading

Use the Think Alouds during the first reading of the text. Notes about the genre may be used during subsequent readings.

Bringing Back Salmon

by Jeffrey Rich

This was a big day for my students at Shasta Union Elementary School in northern California. They would be trying to bring Chinook salmon (shih-NOOK SAM-un) back to nearby Middle Creek.

This creek flows into a big river called the Sacramento. And for 50 years, there had been no salmon at all in the river or the creeks that flow into it. Why? Because people had changed the flow of the river and had polluted the water. Fewer and fewer salmon were able to survive, and finally they all died out.

Since then, people have solved some of the problems that were killing the fish. So now my students would release more than 100 tiny salmon into the creek. They knew that salmon are amazing travelers. The tiny fish, they hoped, would swim about three miles (5 km) down the creek to the Sacramento River. Then they would swim 200 more miles (320 km) to the Pacific Ocean. For two to five years, the salmon would eat and grow. Finally, when they were ready to have young of their own, they'd turn around and swim all the way back upstream to Middle Creek.¹

Or at least, that's what was supposed to happen. No one knew for sure whether our little fish would ever return to where we'd released them.

Cool Eggs, Small Fry

Scientists have always wanted to bring salmon back to this area. So when I had found out they needed some help, I had asked my students if they wanted to join in. The kids said, Yes!

To begin our project, my students visited a fish hatchery. There, they got a bunch of salmon eggs to raise. Salmon can live only in cold water.² So the kids kept the eggs in a tank in a refrigerator. They checked the eggs every day.

Snack in a sac

The kids really enjoyed watching what happened. When the young were ready to hatch, they released an enzyme (EN-zime, a special chemical) that weakened the egg shells. Then the fish wiggled out of their shells and lay on the bottom of the tank.

Baby salmon have yolk sacs attached to their bellies. The sacs are like little bags of high-energy food that the babies use to grow. Finally, when the sacs are gone, the fish are ready to eat tiny animals and plants in the water. When that happened to our fish, we knew it was time to release them![3]

Will it work?

At the creek, the students took one last look at their baby fish. Then they sent them on their way. We watched them swim off and wished them well. Then, on our way back to school, we picked up litter we saw along the creek and the pathway.

Each fall for three years, my students went to the hatchery for more eggs. They eagerly raised and released the baby fish just as they did the first time. Then one day, something wonderful happened. Our fish started coming back! For the first time in 50 years, grown-up salmon were swimming in Middle Creek. The kids had done it! They'd helped to bring these fish back home.

Think Aloud

[3] As I read on, I see that what the author reports about salmon in general helps me know what to expect from this particular group of salmon. For example, he tells me that all salmon lose their yolk sacs. So when he says the students' fish lost their yolk sacs, I know that this is normal. The author says it means it was time to release them.

Genre Study

Nonfiction: Nonfiction about animals is very different from fictional tales about animals. Nonfiction writers have to do research about the animals and give factual information. They cannot just rely on their imaginations or write about make-believe situations or settings.

After Reading

Take Notes: Have students discuss five important facts about salmon that they learned from this selection.

Student Think Aloud

Use Copying Master number 1 to prompt students to think of additional questions they might have about the salmon in the selection and salmon in general.

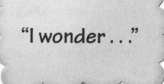

"I wonder . . ."

Think and Respond

1. How are the salmon in the story similar to all salmon? How are they different from other salmon? *Possible responses: They are similar because they live in only cold water, hatch from eggs, use yolk sacs for nourishment, and travel back to where they began. They are different because they were hatched in a refrigerator, cared for by school students, and released into the natural environment.* **Analytical**

2. Why do you think the author and his students took on this project? *Possible response: The creek was no longer polluted and there had not been any salmon in it for 50 years. It was a great way for the students to learn about animals. It was also a way for the class to give back to nature.* **Make Inferences and Analyze**

3. Why do you think the author wanted to share this information about reintroducing the salmon? *Possible responses: He wanted us to realize how changing the environment can affect other living things; he wanted to show how we can help other living things survive.* **Author's Purpose**

Shortstop

by Jerry Spinelli

Genre: Personal Essay

Comprehension Strategy: Generate Questions

Think-Aloud Copying Master number 1

Before Reading

Genre: Tell students that you are going to read aloud a personal essay in which the author recalls what he learned while playing baseball as a boy. Explain that a personal essay is nonfiction writing that reflects an author's personal memories, ideas, or point of view on a particular topic.

Expand Vocabulary: Introduce the following words before reading:

> *shortstop:* the field position in baseball between second and third base
>
> *instinctively:* behaving in a way that is automatic, without thinking
>
> *error:* a poor play made by a fielder in baseball
>
> *console:* to comfort someone who is disappointed

Set a Purpose for Reading: Suggest that students listen carefully to find out what the author learned from playing baseball.

During Reading

Use the Think Alouds during the first reading of the story. Notes about the genre and cultural perspective may be used during subsequent readings.

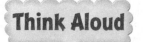

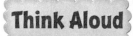

Shortstop

by Jerry Spinelli

From ages eleven to sixteen, if someone asked me what I wanted to be when I grew up, I gave one of two answers: "A baseball player" or "A shortstop."

Major league baseball—that was the life for me. And I wanted to live it only as a shortstop. When I trotted onto a diamond, I instinctively headed for the dusty plain between second and third. I never wanted to play any other position. When we got up sandlot games, no one else occupied shortstop. They knew it was mine.[1]

I was eleven when I first played Little League baseball. To give *as* many kids as possible a chance to participate, the Little League declared that some of us would share uniforms with others. And so the season was exactly half over when I pedaled my bike up to Albert Pascavage's house to pick up his uniform: green socks, green cap, gray woolen shirt, and pants with green trim. I packed my precious cargo into my bike basket and drove it carefully home. I was a member of the Green Sox.

During one game in that half season I played second base—apparently no one told the manager I was going to be a major league shortstop. Our opponent was the Red Sox. The batter hit a ground ball right at me. I crouched, feet spread, glove ready, as I had been taught in the *Times Herald* baseball school. I could hear the ball crunching along the sandy ground. It hit my glove—but not the pocket. Instead it glanced off the fat leather thumb and rolled on behind me.[2]

My first error!

I was heartbroken. I stomped my foot. I pounded my fist into the stupid glove.

When the inning was over and I slunk to the Green Sox bench, the manager was waiting for me. I thought he was going to console me. I thought he would say, "Tough luck, Jerry. Nice try," and then tousle my hair.

That's not what happened.

What he really did was glare angrily at me, and what he really said was, "Don't you ever do that again." He pointed out that while I was standing there pounding my glove, two Red Sox runs had scored. "Next time you miss the ball, you turn around and chase it down. You don't just stand there feeling sorry for yourself. Understand?"

I nodded. And I never forgot.

Respond to the Story: Have students reflect about a difficult lesson they learned and write about it.

Student Think Aloud

Use Copying Master number 1 to prompt students to tell what they found out about the author by reading this personal essay.

"I wonder . . ."

Cultural Perspective

Baseball is an American sport, but it is also popular in many other parts of the world, including Japan, Canada, and Central America.

Think and Respond

1. Do you think you have to be a baseball fan to appreciate this essay? *Possible responses: Yes, because then you will understand why the author loved the game so much. No, because it's really about learning how to handle mistakes.* **Critical**

2. What information does the author include that builds to the idea that the uniform is "precious cargo"? *Possible response: He explains how he had to wait his turn, and how he had to share the uniform with another player. By the time it is his turn he can hardly wait.* **Generate Questions**

3. Why do you think the author wants to share this personal experience? *Accept all reasonable responses. Possible responses: Perhaps he learned something important and wants to pass it on; he wants to show people that when you make a mistake, you shouldn't waste time feeling sorry for yourself.* **Author's Purpose**

How Fisher Went to the Skyland: The Origin of the Big Dipper

an Anishinabe story from the Great Lakes Region

by Joseph Bruchac

Genre: Myth/Legend

Comprehension Strategy: Generate Questions

Think-Aloud Copying Master number 6

Before Reading

Genre: Mention to students that myths and legends, such as the one you are about to read aloud, are stories that have been told and retold for generations. Explain that myths and legends often sound like the history of great people and important events, but they are fiction. Point out that the author, Joseph Bruchac, did not create this story, but is retelling an old story that has been handed down for many years. Inform students that the Anishinabe were also known as Chippewa, a French-Canadian name they did not like, and Ojibwe, an Algonquin word.

Expand Vocabulary: Discuss the following words before reading this legend:

determination: with a firm purpose

fatal: causing death

pity: sadness about another's trouble

Set a Purpose for Reading: Ask students to listen carefully to find out what kind of place Skyland is and why Fisher goes there.

During Reading

Use the Think Alouds during the first reading of the story. Notes about the genre and cultural perspective may be used during subsequent readings.

How Fisher Went to the Skyland: The Origin of the Big Dipper

an Anishinabe story from the Great Lakes Region

by Joseph Bruchac

Fisher was a great hunter. He was not big, but he was known for his <u>determination</u> and was regarded as one with great power. Fisher's son wanted to be a great hunter also. One day the son went out to try to catch something. It was not easy, for the snow was very deep and it was very cold everywhere. In those days it was always winter on the Earth and there was no such thing as warm weather. The son hunted a long time with no luck. Finally, though, he saw a squirrel. As quietly as he could he sneaked up and then pounced, catching the squirrel between his paws. Before he could kill it, though, the squirrel spoke to him.[1]

"Grandson," said the squirrel, "don't kill me. I can give you some good advice."[2]

"Speak then," said the young fisher.

"I see that you are shivering from the cold. If you do what I tell you, we may all enjoy warm weather. Then it will be easy for all of us to find food and not starve as we are doing now."

"Tell me what to do, Grandfather," the young fisher said, letting the squirrel go.

The squirrel climbed quickly up onto a high branch and then spoke again. "Go home and say nothing. Just sit down in your lodge and begin to weep. Your mother will ask you what is wrong, but you must not answer her. If she tries to comfort you or give you food, you must refuse it. When your father comes home, he will ask you why you are weeping. Then you can speak. Tell him the winds are too cold and the snow is too deep. Tell him that he must bring warm weather to the Earth."

So the young fisher went home. He sat in the corner of the lodge and cried. His mother asked what was wrong, but he did not answer. She offered him food, but he pushed it away. When his father returned and saw his only son weeping, he went to his side.

"What is wrong, son?" Fisher said.

Then the young fisher said what the squirrel had told him to say.

Think Aloud

[1] *When I first read this, I wasn't sure if Fisher's son was a man or an animal. But then I figured out he was an animal because he catches the squirrel in his paws.*

Think Aloud

[2] *In myths and legends, animals often behave like humans. It seems perfectly normal that a squirrel starts talking. Squirrel is offering young Fisher his help and advice. I know that animal helpers often appear in Native American legends, so I wonder if there will be other animal helpers, too.*

"I am weeping because the wind is too cold and the snow is too deep. We are all starving because of the winter. I want you to use your powers to bring the warm weather."

"The thing you are asking of me is hard to do," said Fisher, "but you are right. I will do all I can to grant your wish."

Then Fisher had a great feast. He invited all of his friends and told them what he planned to do.

"I am going to go to the place where the skyland is closest to the Earth," he said. "There in the skyland the people have all the warm weather. I intend to go there to bring some of that warm weather back. Then the snow will go away and we will have plenty to eat."

All of Fisher's friends were pleased and offered to go with him. So when Fisher set out, he took the strongest of his friends along. Those friends were Otter, Lynx and Wolverine.

The four of them traveled for a long time through the snow. They went toward the mountains, higher and higher each day. Fisher had with him a pack filled with dried venison and they slept at night buried under the snow. At last, after many, many days, they came to the highest mountain and climbed to its top. Then Fisher took a pipe and tobacco out of his pouch.

"We must offer out smoke to the Four Directions," Fisher said. The four of them smoked and sent their prayers to Gitchee Manitou, asking for success.

The sky was very close above them, but they had to find some way to break through into the land above. "We must jump up," said Fisher. "Who will go first?"

"I will try," said Otter. He leaped up and struck the sky but did not break through. Instead he fell back and slid on his belly all the way to the bottom of the mountain. To this day all otters slide like that in the snow.

"Now it is my turn," said Lynx. He jumped too, striking hard against the sky and falling back unconscious. Fisher tried then, but even he did not have enough power.

"Now it is your turn," said Fisher to Wolverine. "You are the strongest of us all."

Wolverine leaped. He struck hard against the sky and fell back, but he did not give up. He leaped again and again until he made a crack in the sky. Once more he leaped and finally broke through. Fisher jumped through the hole in the sky after him.[3]

The skyland was a beautiful place. It was warm and sunny, and there were plants and flowers of all kinds growing. They could hear the singing of birds all around them, but they could see no people. They went farther and found many long lodges. When they looked inside, they found that there were cages in the lodges. Each cage held a different bird.

"These will make for fine hunting," Fisher said. "Let us set them free."

Quickly Wolverine and Fisher chewed through the rawhide that bound the cages together and freed the birds. The birds all flew down through the hole in the sky. So there are many kinds of birds in the world today.

Wolverine and Fisher now began to make the hole in the skyland bigger. The warmth of the skyland began to fall through the hole and the land below began to grow warmer. The snow began to melt and the grass and plants beneath the snow began to turn green.

But the sky people came out when they saw what was happening. They ran toward Wolverine and Fisher, shouting loudly.

"Thieves," they shouted. "Stop taking our warm weather!"

Wolverine jumped back through the hole to escape, but Fisher kept making the hole bigger. He knew that if he didn't make it big enough, the sky people would quickly close the hole again and it would be winter again in the land below. He chewed the hole larger and larger. Finally, just when the sky people were very close, he stopped.

The hole was big enough for enough warm weather for half of the year to escape through, but it was not big enough for enough warm weather to last all the time. That is why the winter still comes back every year. Fisher knew that the sky people might try to close the hole in the sky. He had to take their attention away from it and so he taunted them.

"I am Fisher, the great hunter," he said. "You cannot catch me." Then he ran to the tallest tree in the skyland. All the sky people ran after him. Just as they were about to grab him, he leaped up

Think Aloud

[3]*I think Wolverine is important because when the first* three *animals fail, I figured, "Well, Wolverine, it's all up to you." After all, whoever started the legend would not have mentioned the animals unless they were important. I know that in legends and fairy tales, things often happen in threes.*

Myth/Legend: In the myths and legends of different cultures, the story often ends with the hero or other main character being changed into a different form, such as a constellation of stars, a tree, or an animal.

into the tree and climbed to the highest branches, where no one could follow.

At first the sky people did not know what to do. Then they began to shoot arrows at him. But Fisher wasn't hurt, for he had a special power. There was only one place on his tail where an arrow could kill him. Finally, though, the sky people guessed where his magic was and shot at that place. An arrow struck the <u>fatal</u> spot. Fisher turned over on his back and began to fall.

But Fisher never struck the Earth. Gitchee Manitou took <u>pity</u> on him because he had kept his promise and done something to help all the people. Gitchee Manitou placed Fisher high up in the sky among the stars.

If you look up into the sky, you can still see him, even though some people call that pattern of stars The Big Dipper. Every year he crosses the sky. When the arrow strikes him, he rolls over onto his back in the winter sky. But when the winter is almost ended, he faithfully turns to his feet and starts out once more on his long journey to bring the warm weather back to the Earth.

Retell the Story: Have students tell the story with a partner, as if they were the descendants of Fisher. Encourage them to pass the myth/legend back and forth, each telling a little part and then letting the other take over, prompting each other to recall what happens next.

Student Think Aloud

Use Copying Master number 6 to prompt students to discuss important events and characters, including the animal helpers, in the story.

"I thought _____ was important in this text because _____."

Cultural Perspective

In Native American myths and legends, animals often play an important role. They can be givers of wisdom or use their power to help people. Sometimes they are tricksters who trick the hero or help him by tricking someone else. Have students give examples of animal tricksters. Ask them what animal they'd use in a trickster tale and explain why.

Think and Respond

1. What do you think the hole in the sky becomes? Why? *Possible response: the sun; because it is round and it makes possible the warm weather* **Analytical**

2. Why could this myth/legend also be called a creation story? *Possible response: It tells how the seasons are created.* **Genre**

3. Why do you think the author decided to write down his retelling of this legend? *Possible responses: because he wanted to make sure that the ancient legends would never be forgotten; because by writing it, he could combine what he had heard with new details from his own imagination* **Author's Purpose**

Helping Hands

by Kathiann M. Kowalski

Genre: Magazine Article

Comprehension Strategy: Generate Questions

Think-Aloud Copying Master number 2

Before Reading

Genre: Tell students that you are going to read aloud a magazine article about how young people help others. Remind them that a magazine article is nonfiction. Point out that, unlike a story, magazine articles almost always include the first and the last names of people. Articles use quotation marks to show what people say about a topic.

Expand Vocabulary: Introduce the following words before reading:

> *ecology:* the study of the relationship between living things and their environment

> *obviously:* very easy to see or understand

> *responsible:* having a certain duty or obligation

> *priceless:* of such great value, it is worth more than money

Set a Purpose for Reading: Ask students to listen to find out the different ways that young volunteers help others.

During Reading

Use the Think Alouds during the first reading of the story. Notes about the genre may be used during subsequent readings.

Helping Hands

by Kathiann M. Kowalski

Alyssa Kovack and Lynn Gusman care about the environment. They like to help people too. Both girls joined the ecology club at Parkview School in Fairview Park, Ohio. Last year the group cleaned up litter. Members also planted a vegetable garden.

"We grew cucumbers, radishes, tomatoes, peppers, string beans, and banana peppers," says Alyssa. "All of our produce was donated to the hunger center."[1]

"We helped feed people who needed food," says Lynn. "It was fun, and it felt good."

Kindness Is Catching

Across the country, young people like Lynn and Alyssa are giving others a helping hand. Obviously, kindness helps other people. Helping others is good for you too!

Society has many problems. But your two hands can make a difference. When you can help even one person, you're not helpless. "It helps to realize that you can do things to help other people," says psychologist Mark Barnett, Ph.D., of Kansas State University. "You're very important to other people.[2]

Acts of kindness connect you to other people. They also help you build your own independence. You learn how to respond when people have a problem. And that helps you grow.

Sometimes a good idea for helping catches on in a huge way. When she was 7 years old, Taylor Crabtree wanted to help kids with cancer. She sold hair clips to raise money and bought teddy bears for children in hospitals.

Volunteers started helping Taylor. Companies gave her money too. In just five years, Taybear Company has given more than 13,000 teddy bears to sick children.

Starting Out Small

Of course, you don't need to organize a huge project to make a difference. "Even small acts of kindness can be very powerful stuff," says Barnett. "If there's a family that's needy or a child

Think Aloud

[1] *I made a connection here because I have taken part in efforts to help the hungry. There are many ways to help the hungry, such as donating canned food to a food bank or giving cash to a volunteer organization. In this article, the writer reports that some people help by growing food and giving it away.*

Think Aloud

[2] *Here the writer talks directly to the reader, pointing out that each of us can help. She also quotes an expert, someone who knows a lot about why people do things. This helps her prove the point she is trying to make and makes it even more convincing.*

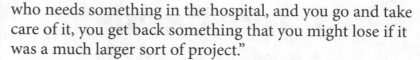

who needs something in the hospital, and you go and take care of it, you get back something that you might lose if it was a much larger sort of project."

"I raked leaves for some elderly people," says Eric McGinnis. "It made them happy, and they were glad it was done."

Eric and members of his scout troop also painted a fence for an older couple. The couple was grateful. And the boys had fun working together.

Rachel Aldrich has also done volunteer work with her scout troop. Last summer, the girls went to a homeless shelter. The troop spent a day cleaning and organizing clothes and toys for children.

"There were jobs at the shelter that just needed extra people to help out with them," says Rachel. "It made me feel good to know I made a difference. Helping people out is the right thing to do."[3]

Saying Yes

Getting involved in community service can be as simple as saying yes when someone asks for help. Mark Goins babysits preschool children every Sunday at his church. The teacher running the program needed helpers, so Mark agreed.

"Some of my friends go there too and help out," says Mark. "It's fun to be with them over the weekend." He also thinks volunteering helps kids learn to be <u>responsible</u>.

Saying yes to helping others is always easy. "It's not fun sometimes going to a hospital or a nursing home and seeing people who are struggling," says Barnett. But your visit can help someone feel better. You grow closer to other people, too, and that feels good.

A Family Affair

When families volunteer together, they can grow closer to each other. Older kids can be role models for younger brothers and sisters. And everyone can have fun.

Brianna Mayer's family signed up to help when her church served a Thanksgiving dinner to needy people. Brianna set tables and poured drinks. "The volunteer work provided a good meal for some hungry people," Brianna says.

Helping out at home counts too. John Moser often helps watch his little niece, Lily, when his older sister works. "You have to keep track of where she is," says John. "She moves fast." And if John ever has children, he says, "I'll know better how to handle them."

Feeling Good

"The best thing about volunteering is that you feel good about what you just did," says Brianna. That boost in self-esteem is <u>priceless</u>.

Alyssa agrees. "I personally feel happy and proud," she says, "and that definitely is a plus when you volunteer."

"It makes me feel good to know that I'm doing something for someone else," says Eric. He encourages other kids to volunteer too. "You'll feel good about it, and you might make friends."

Take Notes: Ask students to list and briefly describe the different types of volunteering mentioned in the article. Direct them to generate who, what, when, where and how questions to guide them.

Student Think Aloud

Use Copying Master number 2 to prompt students to tell what they found out about the topic and the volunteers by reading this article.

"I made a connection when . . ."

Think and Respond

1. What types of volunteering have you already seen in action, taken part in, or read about? Which of these would you like to try? *Accept all reasonable responses, encouraging students to fully explain their responses.* **Analytical/ Critical**

2. Why do you think the writer included quotations from young volunteers? *Possible responses: She wanted to make the article more interesting; she wanted the young volunteers to explain in their own words why they help others.* **Genre**

3. The author admits that there are many problems in the world. Why do you think she wrote about these volunteers and their various activities? *Accept all reasonable responses. Possible responses: She wants to show that there is always some way to help solve any problem; everybody can help, whether in big ways or small, as an individual or as part of a team.* **Author's Purpose**

THE MAGICAL HORSE

by Laurence Yep

Genre: Fantasy

Comprehension Strategy: Summarize

Think-Aloud Copying Master number 3

Before Reading

Genre: Review the key elements of a fantasy with students. Explain that a fantasy has invented characters, events, or other elements that are not possible in the real world.

Expand Vocabulary: Discuss the following words before reading:

> *saliva:* the liquid made by glands in the mouth to help digest food
>
> *dabbler:* someone who does something carelessly or without taking It serlously
>
> *awe:* a feeling of amazement and respect
>
> *possession:* something that somebody owns
>
> *vandalized:* deliberately destroyed or damaged property

Set a Purpose for Reading: Invite students to listen to find out where the magical horse comes from and how its magic changes people's lives.

During Reading

Use the Think Alouds during the first reading of the story. Notes about the genre and cultural perspective may be used during subsequent readings.

THE MAGICAL HORSE

by Laurence Yep

Many years ago there lived a wonderful painter. No one could paint animals as he could. Ducks flew from his paintings. Monkeys leaped from trees. Tigers bounded.

Despite his skill, no one would buy his paintings because he mixed his paints with the saliva of old men. He didn't care, because none of his own paintings satisfied him. "My hands chase what my heart admires," he would often say, "and always in vain."[1]

As a result, he never painted the animal he loved the most: the horse. "To paint a horse, I must paint beauty and nobility itself, but I am merely a clumsy dabbler whose paintings have no spirit."

He put it off for years, trying to paint instead what he called the lesser animals and the lesser virtues. One day he looked in the mirror and saw the reflection of an old man. With a shock, he realized that he did not have to collect anyone else's spit anymore, he could use his own.

He had a boy named Sunny, his only relation, who had been born late in his life before his wife had died. He called Sunny in now and announced his decision. "I have waited all these years for my skill to match my love; and now I have almost run out of time. Though I am still a hopeless bungler, today I shall begin my painting of a horse."

It was not to be any horse, though, but a horse that could run a thousand miles without growing tired. Day after day he sketched, until his studies covered the room in layers. And day by day, he and Sunny grew poorer. They had to sell everything— all his paintings and then their furniture and even the house.

Still he kept on, until one day he announced he was ready to paint a thousand-mile horse. Standing before the long, narrow canvas, he squatted down as if he were actually on a saddle. He forgot about the cold and his hunger and his many years, and his brush flew. Sunny begged him to rest, but the painter ignored his son as he painted a snow-white mare that seemed almost to fly across the plains. At the end of the day, the painter set his brush down and announced that he was nearly done.[2]

Think Aloud

[1] *Saliva? These first two paragraphs really show an interesting contrast between the magnificence of the paintings and the unexpected material used to create them. It reminds me that a good story, like art, isn't just about pretty things, but about all kinds of imaginative details.*

Think Aloud

[2] *The author is painting such a vivid picture in my mind here! I can picture the artist crouching down and concentrating. I can see his son coming into the room again and again, trying to get him to rest or eat. I know how tired the artist must look, getting pale and weak from lack of rest.*

Sunny stared in <u>awe</u> at his father's masterpiece. "What more could you do to the painting? Every stroke is perfect."

"It needs one thing more," the painter said, and sat down weakly. "But first swear that you won't sell this painting until it is time."

When Sunny promised, his father silently held up his arms for Sunny to lift him. "But how will I know?" Sunny asked.

"The painting will tell you." The painter looked at the magnificent horse upon the narrow rectangle and then heaved a large sigh. With that last breath, his spirit left his body and passed into the painting itself.

Sadly, Sunny lowered his father's now lifeless body onto the floor and then went begging for the money to bury his father.

"It's your father's own fault that you have no money," the neighbors said smugly.

So the faithful son had to sell himself to a farmer for the necessary money.

When he had buried his father, he moved into the farmer's barn. His one <u>possession</u> was the painting, which he put up on the wall. Staring up at the horse, Sunny wished that he could carry on his father's work, but he knew that he had not inherited his father's skill. "My hands can never pursue what my heart desires," Sunny said to himself. "But his memory will live as long as I do." So that first night, he begged some incense sticks from the farmer.

"It won't make the barn smell any better." The farmer laughed.

"This is for my father's spirit, which he gave to the painting," Sunny said. And the farmer was so ashamed that he provided Sunny with incense sticks.

As the boy sat with his body aching from the hard work and eating his cold rice, he gazed up at the painting. His father had caught the horse as if it were suspended upon one hoof. And as he watched, the horse's sides seemed to heave in the moonlight—as if it were breathing in the incense. On a whim, Sunny set out feed for his painted horse just as he did for the other animals.

He slept among the beasts for warmth, so he was not surprised when he felt an animal's warm breath blow on him. When a nose nudged him, he sat up irritated, intending to shove the creature away, but his hand paused in the air.

By the light of the moon, he saw a silvery horse standing over him. He looked over at the wall where the painting had been and saw that the canvas was empty. The next thing he knew, he was on the back of the horse, his hands clinging to the flying mane, the horse's hooves booming rhythmically along a road that gleamed like a silver ribbon winding up into the sky. And his sadness evaporated like rain hitting hot stones.

The next morning, when Sunny woke up, he found the feed was gone. "So it was real," Sunny said. "It wasn't a dream."

Each night after that, he would take his meal with the magical horse; and each night he rode the marvelous beast to wherever he wanted, because even great distances melted beneath those miraculous hooves.

One evening Sunny took it into his head to see the king's palace, and they galloped up to the very walls of the great palace with its golden roof tiles.

Now the prince happened to be looking out his window and saw Sunny and the white horse flash past in the blink of an eye; and in that same blink, the prince wanted a horse just like that.

So the next morning he went to his father, the king. "I have one of everything in my collection of wonders. I have a phoenix's egg. I have the whiskers from the chin of a dragon king. But I do not have a thousand-mile horse."

"You have plenty of horses in the stable already," the king argued.

"None of them can travel as far and as fast as a thousand-mile horse," the prince insisted.[3]

So the king, who could never say no to his son, offered six hundred pieces of silver to the person who brought him such a magical horse.

The farmer shook his head when he heard the news. "It's too bad that you don't have a real thousand-mile horse instead of a painted one."

Sunny, though, wasn't sorry at all, for if he were to sell his painting, he would miss his midnight rides.

People hunted all over for a thousand-mile horse. The honest ones searched by day, but there was a thief who looked by night. He sneaked through the forts and looked at the cavalry chargers. He stole onto the big farms and examined all the animals. Nowhere did he find a thousand-mile horse.

Think Aloud

[3] I notice how dialogue is used to move the story forward. The author uses a conversation between the king and the prince to set up a situation that connects to Sunny. Dialogue helps move along the plot, and gives clues about how characters think and behave.

Then one night as he was leaving a stable, he heard the drumming of hooves. He looked up just in time to see a boy riding a gleaming horse; and then they were gone in a single breath. However, he had time to see that the horse's tail was burned. At first he thought he was dreaming; but then in the moonlight he saw the hoofprints.

Eagerly, the thief followed the trail. It took many days, and several times he lost the tracks in all the traffic in the road, but he always managed to find them again until he reached the farm.

Hiding in a bush, he scratched his head in puzzlement. "The tracks come from there, but what is a thousand-mile horse doing in a miserable place like that?" Even so, he kept a watch on the place.

Sure enough, the magical horse appeared with the rising of the moon. In the time it took the thief to gulp, the horse and rider had vanished from sight. A while later, they reappeared, leaped over the wall, and entered the barn.

Using all his skill, the thief sneaked into the farm and entered the barn. He saw Sunny asleep among the animals, but there was no thousand-mile horse.

Suddenly the thief noticed the painting. An incense stick had burned part of the canvas near the horse's tail. He realized, then, that the horse in the painting was magical. He was just about to snatch the painting from the wall when he heard a rooster crow, and the farm began to stir. Hurriedly the thief fled.

The next day he carefully asked questions around the neighborhood before he visited the farm. "I have always wanted a painting by that master. I'll give you eighty cash," the thief offered.

His price made the farmer's jaw drop open. "Sell it," he urged Sunny.

However, Sunny refused. "A promise is a promise."

"That's what I get for trying to be honest," the thief muttered. He went as far as his bush and dropped out of sight to wait until everyone had gone to the fields. Then he sneaked back into the barn and stole the painting.

He hid in an abandoned shack until nightfall and then hung up the painting of the thousand-mile horse. He planned to ride the horse to the palace that very night.

When the moon shone through the doorway of the shack, the horse reappeared, but he seemed puzzled to see the thief

and not the painter's son. When the thief grasped the horse's bridle, the beast reared and kicked, and it was all the thief could do to keep out of the way of the flailing hooves.

"Stop that," he ordered the horse, "or I'll burn the painting tomorrow morning."

The next instant, the horse was still, trembling where it stood. Hardly daring to believe his luck, the thief took down the now-empty scroll and led the creature outside.

Rolling up the scroll, the thief scrambled onto the magical horse's back. "Take me to the king's palace," he commanded.

The horse thundered off. Trees flashed by in the wink of an eye. The wind of their passage tore the scroll from the thief's hand. "Stop. Go back," the thief cried.

The horse only galloped faster, and the world—houses and hills, streams and valleys—whizzed by in a blur. If I fall off now, the thief thought, I'll break every bone in my body. With that in mind, the desperate thief grabbed the whipping mane in both hands and held on for dear life.

When the horse finally slowed down, the thief saw that they were not at the king's palace but in some garden where rocks rose upward like mountains from pools fashioned like miniature seas.

Ahead of them, through the moonlit trees, he saw a magnificent mansion. Everything seemed hushed and still. Even his mount's hooves hardly made a sound.

He rubbed his hands gleefully. "This horse is worth more than six hundred pieces of silver. I can ride it to faraway places to loot and be back home the very same night so no one could ever suspect me. Whatever my heart wants, my hands can take."

Jumping off the horse, he tied it to a bush and patted its neck. "I'm going to keep you for myself." And he sneaked inside the mansion.

Now Sunny had been terribly upset when he found the painting missing. He had searched all over the farm, and when he could find no trace of it, he had run away to hunt for it in the countryside. He looked everywhere until he finally lay down, exhausted, and fell asleep.

When he first felt the warm breath blowing at his ear, he thought he was dreaming, but when he felt the muzzle nudging him, he sat up joyfully and saw the magical white horse. It had managed to pull itself free. Climbing onto the magical creature's back, he let himself be carried to a tree not very far from the bush where the thief had hidden. In the branches where it had been blown, he found the scroll.

Once the scroll was safely rolled up and tucked under his arm, he told the horse to take him back to the farm. Instead, the horse took him in the opposite direction until they saw the king's palace in the distance. The royal roof was a gleaming red dot when the sun rose. Immediately, Sunny plopped down on the road as the horse disappeared from the road. Hurriedly he unrolled the scroll to see that the horse had reappeared once again in the painting.

Sorrowfully, Sunny remembered his father's words then. He knew that this was the sign that he should sell the painting now.

It took most of the morning to reach the palace itself. When he reached the gates, he found the whole place in an uproar because someone had <u>vandalized</u> a very rare painting.

At first, the gatekeeper didn't want to admit the ragged boy who claimed to have a thousand-mile horse, but since the gatekeeper was under orders to admit anyone who might satisfy the prince's whim, he eventually let Sunny in.

Sunny was passed from one reluctant servant to another until he was led into the throne room, where the king and prince were both examining the ruined painting.

"If this is the work of a vandal," the prince observed, "then it's a very talented vandal. This thief is lifelike."

The king was tugging at his beard. "It is not the thief's talent but his intentions that worry me. If someone could get past all my guards to do this, he could get into my very bedroom to kill me."

As Sunny waited to be introduced to the king, he looked up at the long scroll. His father, he thought, had painted far better, but it was a good old-fashioned landscape of a mansion nestled within an elaborate garden.

The king turned to his counselors and his generals. "Find out who this is, and find out at once." And he stepped back to point at one corner of the painting.

There, near a bush in the garden, was the thief. His mouth was open and his hands were pressed flat as if he were calling for help from the other side of a window.

"That's the man who tried to buy my painted horse," Sunny gasped.

Genre Study

Fantasy: In a fantasy, the lives and fortunes of characters can change suddenly. Sunny grows up in a comfortable home, loses almost every-thing, but ends up rich and living in a palace. Often, though not always, a fantasy ends with the main character living happily ever after.

All eyes turned to Sunny, much to his discomfort. "Do you know this man?" the king demanded.

So Sunny told everything he knew—from his father's painting of the horse to its loss and recovery.

"Let me see the painting," the king commanded.

When the scroll was unrolled, his eyes gleamed appreciatively. "Your father was truly a master. I can believe that this painting comes to life. The horse almost seems to be breathing right now before my very eyes." He looked back at the picture of the thief. "And if a painted horse can come to life, then perhaps a live thief can become a painting."

So the king ordered Sunny's painting to be hung up in the garden, and that evening everyone gathered to watch. As the first rays of moonlight touched the painting, the magical horse leaped to the ground, where it stood, stamping its hooves.

First the king and then his son took a quick canter and pronounced themselves satisfied that this was indeed a thousand-mile horse. They not only gave Sunny a large sum of money but invited him to live in the palace. So, after buying his freedom, Sunny settled down to a comfortable life.

And whenever the prince lacked the time or the desire for a gallop, he would send the horse to the painter's son, and Sunny would once again take long rides in the moonlight.

Retell the Story: Invite students to retell the story from the point of view of another character in the story, such as the prince, the farmer, or the thief.

Student Think Aloud

Use Copying Master number 3 to prompt students to describe some of the scenes or details that they mentally pictured from the story.

"I was able to picture in my mind . . ."

Cultural Perspective

In Chinese art, the horse is a symbol of strength and speed. In 1974, archaeologists in China uncovered life-size terra-cotta statues of horses and warriors. The sculptures had been hidden from view for more than 2,000 years!

Think and Respond

1. Why do you think there was an image of the thief in the damaged painting? What makes you think so? *Possible responses: He had tried to steal it and got trapped instead; the author says that his hands are pushed flat and his mouth is open as if he were calling for help.* **Inferential**

2. How is this like other fantasies you have heard or read? *Possible responses: They all tell about good people who go from being poor to rich or from unlucky to lucky; they all include animals or objects that have magic powers.* **Genre**

3. Do you think the author has more in mind than just to share an interesting story? *Possible responses: Yes, because he also shows how humble the great artist is, how the thief is punished, and how Sunny keeps his promise to his father. No, because it is mostly about events that could not happen in real life, but it is very entertaining.* **Author's Purpose**

SLED DOGS: Arctic Athletes

by Elizabeth Ring

Genre: Nonfiction

Comprehension Strategy: Generate Questions

Think-Aloud Copying Master number 1

Before Reading

Genre: Explain to students that you are going to read aloud a nonfiction selection about arctic sled dogs and the ways people have come to depend on them over time. Mention that since this is nonfiction, the author will give a realistic description of these animals and the setting in which they work.

Expand Vocabulary: Introduce the following words before reading:

> *desperately:* overwhelmed with worry
>
> *blizzard:* a severe snowstorm that makes it difficult or impossible to see
>
> *frantic:* excited, fearful, and in a hurry all at once
>
> *fierce:* powerful, even violent

Set a Purpose for Reading: Encourage students to read to learn about arctic dogs and the way they help people.

During Reading

Use the Think Alouds during the first reading of the story. Notes about the genre and cultural perspective may be used during subsequent readings.

SLED DOGS: Arctic Athletes

by Elizabeth Ring

A half hour out of Crazy Horse Camp near Prudhoe Bay, north of the Arctic Circle, the dogsled sped over hard-packed snow. There was no hint of a coming storm. Then, without warning, the sled was swallowed up in cold, stinging fog—a swirling Alaskan "whiteout."

Slim Randles's dog team kept running. Tanya, a big silver-gray dog, and Wolf, her strong black-coated partner, were in the lead. Behind them ran eight other dogs, pulling the sled steadily along the slick trail. The man rode standing on the back of the sled's runners.

Randles, a newspaper reporter and experienced dogsled driver, had been in whiteouts before. When the icy fog swept down on the sled, he knew a snowstorm could follow. Then the storm hit. Blinding snow whooshed up, down, and from every side. The winds made the already below-zero temperature feel at least thirty degrees colder. Quickly, Randles turned the dogs back toward camp, hoping <u>desperately</u> that the team would get there before the <u>blizzard</u> got too bad.[1]

"Hy-a-a-ah!" Randles yelled, urging the dogs to go faster.

Randles could feel his breath start to freeze on his face. In minutes, he could barely open his mouth to shout commands to Tanya and Wolf. It hardly mattered. How could he direct the dogs if he could not see a foot in front of him? All he could do was crouch down, cling to the driving bow of the sled, and trust that Tanya's and Wolf's "dog sense" would guide them back to camp.

The dogs plowed ahead. On and on they went through the raging storm and the fast-deepening snow. Randles became more and more certain that they were off track. It would not be the first time his team had lost its way.

Then, quite suddenly, the whole team stopped short. Randles could not believe his dogs would quit on him this way. He felt his way forward in the swirling snow until he reached the head of the column of dogs. Tanya, usually reliable, was furiously digging a hole in a snowbank, as if refusing to go a step farther.

<u>Frantic</u>, Randles yanked on Tanya's collar, to get her going. But she refused to stop digging. Then Randles looked up, peering through the whiteness. Right in front of him was a porch. His dogs had brought the sled straight to the camp door.

Genre Study

Nonfiction: When nonfiction writers relate information about animals they focus on facts and descriptive details. In nonfiction, animals are portrayed as they really act.

Think Aloud

[1] *I wonder what Slim Randles is doing out in the middle of this storm. I will reread the first paragraphs to make sure I caught every detail. Oh, that's right. There was no hint of a coming storm. The author says that Randles has been in whiteouts before. I wonder how he will handle it this time.*

Randles thawed out indoors. The dogs needed no shelter. Unharnessed and tied down for the night, they all dug holes for themselves in the snow. They curled up into tight balls of fur. They looped their tails over their noses, shielding their lungs from the frigid air. Bedded down under a blanket of snow, the dogs were as snug as if they were housed in an igloo.[2]

Arctic dogs like Tanya and Wolf have helped people through fierce arctic winters for thousands of years. When did these hardy dogs first join forces with humans? Nobody knows exactly. Historians think it may have been about four thousand years ago, among the Eskimos of Siberia.

All anyone knows for sure is that at some time arctic dogs became people's companions and partners. They pulled sleds and herded reindeer. They helped in hunting wild animals such as seals and polar bears. They guarded camps against wolves and bears. In summer, they hauled flat sleighs over the tundra (arctic soil) and trotted along riverbanks pulling boats up- and downstream. At times they carried packs on their backs.[3]

Eskimos of eastern Siberia, Alaska, Greenland, and the Canadian Arctic were all nomads at one time. They moved from one place to another instead of living in permanent villages. Dogs (some crossbred with wolves) accompanied the migrant tribes.

In time, arctic people came to depend for their lives on their dogs. The Eskimos matched their smartest and strongest dogs to breed smart, sturdy pups. They also bred dogs that were especially good at scenting and tracking seals, polar bears, and musk-oxen. Much later, when dogsled racing became a popular sport, the dogs were bred (by both Eskimos and other people) for speed as well as intelligence, strength, and endurance.

Take Notes: Remind students that even though Randles is a newspaper reporter, he can hardly take notes during a whiteout. Invite students to take notes for him. Encourage them to include "who, what, when, where, why" details that would go into a news story about arctic dogs.

Student Think Aloud

"I wonder . . ."

Use Copying Master number 1 to prompt students to share questions they had about the selection and how readers can look for answers in the text.

Cultural Perspective

The Eskimo culture is not just one group of people, but includes many different groups, including Yu'pik, Inuit, and Inupiaq. Have students research which tribes still exist. Investigate where they live and which part of the culture is evident today.

Think and Respond

1. How would life have been different for arctic people if they had not joined forces with these dogs? *Possible responses: They would not have been able to travel in snow; they might not have found enough food without help from the dogs.* **Analytical**

2. Do you think it would be better if the author had started off with facts about arctic dogs rather than the snowstorm adventure? *Possible responses: Yes, then you would have a better understanding of why these dogs knew what to do during the whiteout. No, telling us about Tanya, Wolf, and the exciting adventure makes you care about these dogs and want to learn more about them.* **Genre**

3. Why do you think the author wrote this nonfiction article about dogs? *Accept all reasonable responses. Possible responses: The author wanted people to know what a fascinating history arctic dogs have; she wanted to remind people that dogs are not always just pets, but they also help people.* **Author's Purpose**

Pecos Bill Invents the Lariat

a tall tale from Texas

by James Cloyd Bowman

Genre: Tall Tale

Comprehension Strategy: Analyze Story Structure

Think-Aloud Copying Master number 4

Before Reading

Genre: Tell students that tall tales, such as the one you are about to read, are exaggerated stories based on America's frontier days. Usually the setting of a tall tale is the wilderness, the characters are rugged individuals, and the plot is based on a farfetched adventure.

Expand Vocabulary: Introduce the following words and phrases before reading the tall tale:

> *eating out of someone's hand:* doing whatever someone asks
>
> *attempt:* to try
>
> *forearm:* the part of the human arm between the elbow and the wrist
>
> *noose:* a loop tied with a knot at the end of a rope

Set a Purpose for Reading: Invite students to listen to the story to find out why it qualifies as a tall tale.

During Reading

Use the Think Alouds during the first reading of the story. Notes about the genre and cultural perspective may be used during subsequent readings. Emphasize the humor and exaggerated details during the read aloud.

Pecos Bill Invents the Lariat

a tall tale from Texas
by James Cloyd Bowman

All the men of the I. X. L. were eating out of Pecos Bill's hand within less than a week after he arrived. He took to the life of a cowboy like a duck to water. He learned their best tricks, then went on to do better. Gun Smith and Chuck and the rest were very soon like children before him. Among themselves, they bragged about their noble deeds; but when Pecos was around, they couldn't help thinking that they were mere bridled cayuses.[1]

He could stand on the ground beside a broncho, turn an air flop, and land astride the pony before it had time to tighten a muscle. He could ride bareback without a bridle. He could urge his pony at top speed over ground so rough and uneven that Gun Smith and the others were afraid even to attempt it with bit and saddle. And he was so casual and modest about everything he did that they thought Pecos the eighth wonder of the world. Almost at once he was full of ideas. And what ideas!

Up to Pecos Bill's day, when a man wanted to capture a horse or a steer, he would lay a piece of rope down on the ground, make a loop in one end of it, sit down behind a tree or a blind, and by laying a bait, try to coax the wild critter to step within the loop. He would then jerk sharply on the rope, and perhaps one time in a dozen, if he was lucky, he would succeed in making a catch. It was no uncommon thing for a man to wait around and lose an entire month's time without laying hold of a single animal.[2]

"Well, this sort of thing has got to be changed," said Pecos Bill to himself when no one was near to hear him. "A man can't be expected to waste his entire lifetime catching a single horse or cow."

Without further delay, Pecos got hold of the longest piece of rope he could find around the ranch, and began to throw it through the air. Next he rode off alone where the others could not see what he was doing. After three days of constant practice, he found that he could lasso almost anything. He was limited only by the reach of his line.

Pecos Bill would just make a large loop in one end of his rope, swing it wildly about his head three or four times, and then, with a quick flip of his forearm and wrist, send it flying

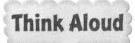

Think Aloud

[1] I figured out that I.X.L. must be a ranch because the names of ranches are often abbreviated. I also use what I know to figure out that because cayuses wear bridles, they are probably horses.

Think Aloud

[2] At first it seems like the author is writing in a serious tone of voice but I think he's really pulling my leg—so to speak! Surely it can't take a man an entire month to catch one animal. I think the author is setting up the story to explain why Pecos Bill needed to find a faster way to catch animals.

Genre Study

Tall Tale: The author of this tall tale sometimes uses a serious tone of voice, as if the incredible events were perfectly normal.

like a bullet. And as he grew more and more skilled, he added rapidly to the length of his rope.

As soon as he was entirely sure of himself, Pecos asked the boys to come out and let him show them his new invention.

"See that roan steer across there? That's Old Crook-horn, our wildest critter, ain't it?" Pecos asked quietly.

Before anyone was aware of what he was doing, Pecos had whirled his loop about his head and had sent it so fast in the direction of the four-year-old, that the eye could scarcely follow it.

In an instant the old steer began to jump and bellow, and Pecos Bill began to tow in the rope. Soon the astonished steer stood with lowered head before the even more surprised cowboys.

Not content with this great skill, Pecos began practicing from horseback.

In another week, he again called his cowboys out to see what he could do. They watched, with popping eyes, as he gave his rope a double turn around his saddle-bow. He then started his broncho at a hard gallop. They saw him quickly approach a rather tall, scraggly mesquite tree, whirl his loop wildly about his head and then fling it into the air. When he dragged a great hawk down from the topmost branch with the <u>noose</u> about its neck, the men were unable to believe their eyes.

"What sort o' wonder worker is this anyway?" they asked each other. "No human could ever throw the rope like that!"

Then Pecos Bill showed the men how it was done, and after two or three months of hard practice, each of them was able to make frequent catches at a distance of from ten to not more than twenty feet.

In the meantime, Pecos Bill had become dissatisfied with the fact that he couldn't find a longer rope. So he began to braid himself a cowhide lariat. This is how he went to work. First he looked up some old horned steers that had lived so many years within the depths of the trees that there were green algae on their backs—moss-backs, sure enough. What's more, these steers were so old their faces were gray and wrinkled.

Whenever Pecos Bill got hold of one of these old fellows, he first loosened the hide behind the ears. He then grasped the steer by the tail and with a flip of his wrists and forearm and a wild yowl, he frightened the animal so that it jumped out of its skin.[3] The tough hides of these old moss-backs were just what Pecos needed.

Think Aloud

[3] Now I know this is definitely a tall tale! Steers can't jump out of their own skin! I've heard that phrase before, but never in the way this author uses it.

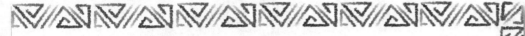

Three or four years later when he had it finished, his loyal ranchers declared on all sides that the lariat was as long as the equator, and that Pecos could lasso anything this side of China.

It was thus that Pecos Bill solved one of the problems that had worried cowhands and their bosses for years.

After Reading

Retell the Story: Ask students to retell the story using as much exaggeration as they can while trying to keep a straight face.

Student Think Aloud

Use Copying Master number 4 to prompt students to explain how they figured out a difficult passage, word, or other detail in the tall tale.

"I figured out _____ because . . ."

Cultural Perspective

A famous African American hero of tall tales was John Henry. He was a railroad builder who died after proving he could work faster than a steam driver. Some say the tall tale was based on a real person, but no one knows for sure.

Think and Respond

1. What difficult task led Pecos Bill to invent the lariat? *Possible responses: A man had to lay down a piece of rope on the ground, make a loop in it, and wait for a critter to step into it. It could take an entire lifetime to catch a single horse or cow.* **Analytical**

2. How does this tall tale compare with others you have read or heard? *Possible responses: It mixes exaggeration with a serious tone. It tells about something that never happened as if it were historical fact. It features a larger-than-life character. It is set in the American wilderness.* **Genre**

3. What is the purpose of this tall tale? *Possible responses: to entertain and amuse; to add to the tradition of telling tales about the character Pecos Bill.* **Author's Purpose**

Notes on the Art of Poetry

by Dylan Thomas

Genre: Poem

Poetic Element: Figurative Language

Comprehension Strategy: Monitor Comprehension

Think-Aloud Copying Master number 5

Before Reading

Genre: Tell students that the poem you are going to read aloud celebrates the power of poetry itself. Explain that this poem is written in free verse. It does not rhyme, and the line length varies.

Expand Vocabulary: Before reading the poem aloud, present the following words to students:

> *goings-on:* events, activities
>
> *staggering:* causing great amazement
>
> *oddity:* something that seems strange or unusual

Set a Purpose for Reading: Ask students to listen to the way the poet compares poetry to extraordinary happenings. Point out that there are many literary devices such as assonance, consonance, repetition, and comparisons in the poem.

During Reading

For the first reading, read without stopping. Use a tone that reflects the thrill the poet felt when he first discovered the imaginative delight of poetry. On subsequent readings, discuss the Think Aloud and encourage students to draw connections between the poet's feelings and their own.

Notes on the Art of Poetry

by Dylan Thomas

I could never have dreamt that there were such <u>goings-on</u>

in the world between the covers of books,

such sandstorms and ice blasts of words, , ,[1]

such <u>staggering</u> peace, such enormous laughter,

such and so many blinding bright lights, , ,

splashing all over the pages

in a million bits and pieces

all of which were words, words, words,

and each of which were alive forever

in its own delight and glory and <u>oddity</u> and light.

Think Aloud

[1] *I notice that the poet compares words to a blast of ice. I know what he means. When I read, a surprising line can stop me cold and a new idea can be as refreshing as ice water on a hot day!*

Genre Study

Poem: Free verse does not rhyme, follow a regular rhythm, or use lines that are all the same length. This poem has a natural sound to it, as if the poet had written it in one burst of inspiration or feeling.

Set a Purpose for Rereading: Ask students to discuss the figurative language used in the poem and give examples. Have the students write their own free verse poem. Encourage them to use some of the devices discussed.

Student Think Aloud

Use Copying Master number 5 to prompt students to discuss which phrase or line best captures the power of poetry. Encourage them to give reasons for their answer.

"I noticed the author used . . ."

Think and Respond

1. How does this poem reflect the poet's love of reading? *Possible response: The poet compares the words in books to living things or different places. The images he uses are fascinating, not scary.* **Analytical**

2. How can this be a poem if it does not rhyme? *Possible responses: The poet uses repetition, imagery, and other poetic elements. Poems do not have to rhyme.* **Genre**

3. Why do you think the poet wrote about poetry itself? *Accept reasonable responses. Possible responses: He wanted to show how much poetry means to him. He wanted to show people who do not like poetry how exciting it can be.* **Author's Purpose**

I Made a Perpetual Motion Machine

by Jack Prelutsky

Genre: Poem

Poetic Element: Rhythm

Comprehension Strategy: Generate Questions

Think-Aloud Copying Master number 6

Before Reading

Genre: Tell students that the poem you are going to read aloud uses rhythm in a very clever way, to imitate a machine. Remind students that some poems use rhythm to create a whimsical mood.

Expand Vocabulary: Before reading the poem aloud, review the following words with students:

>*perpetual:* lasting for all time
>
>*discarded:* thrown away
>
>*unabated:* as strong as ever
>
>*precise:* exact

Set a Purpose for Reading: Ask students to listen to the way the poem imitates the sound and rhythm of a machine.

During Reading

For the first reading, read the poem without pausing, using a lighthearted tone of voice and a lively rhythm. Emphasize the surprise ending of the poem (I slipped and fell in . . .). On subsequent readings, pause to discuss the Think Aloud and genre note.

I Made a Perpetual Motion Machine

by Jack Prelutsky

I made a perpetual motion machine,
the only one anyone ever has seen.
I put it together without any plan,
and so I was more than surprised when it ran.

I made it of skateboards and bicycle parts,
discarded pianos and old shopping carts.[1]
I didn't write down how I did what I did,
I don't even know how I put on the lid.

Its power apparently hasn't a source,
not gas or electric, atomic or horse.
Yet somehow it's run unabated for years,
without any wear on the pistons or gears.

I've recently wished my amazing device
would shut itself down and not be so precise.
It's all on account of an unforeseen turn
that finds me expressing increasing concern.

I freely confess I'm not having much fun,
I'm sleeping too fast, and I eat on the run.
I slipped and fell in while attempting to clean
my perfect perpetual motion machine.

Set a Purpose for Rereading: Have students listen again to the poem to locate rhyming pairs, and to tap out or vocally imitate the rhythm.

Student Think Aloud

Use Copying Master number 6 to prompt students to discuss the rhyme, rhythm, humor, and other elements found in the poem.

"I thought _____ was important in this text because . . ."

Think and Respond

1. What are some of the reasons this machine could exist only in the imagination? *Possible responses: It is made out of unusual things that do not necessarily go together. It has no power source, but started running by itself and will not stop. It has trapped the poet inside of it.* **Inferential**

2. Why Is rhythm so effective in this poem? *Possible response: The poet uses rhythmic language to imitate the sound and motion of a machine.* **Poetic Element**

3. Why do you think the poet wrote this poem? *Possible responses: to show the power of the imagination; to tell a joke about a situation that gets out of control* **Author's Purpose**

Search for the Past

from *Dig This! How Archaeologists Uncover Our Past*

by Michael Avi-Yonah

Genre: Informational Article

Comprehension Strategy: Summarize

Think-Aloud Copying Master number 1

Before Reading

Genre: Tell students that nonfiction selections often explore one idea or topic in great detail. Point out that the article they will hear explains what archaeology is and how scientists use it to learn about ancient civilizations.

Expand Vocabulary: To help students better understand archaeology, introduce and explain the following words:

> *preservation:* the saving of something of historic value
>
> *field:* an activity or subject
>
> *accumulation:* a number of objects that have been gathered over a long time
>
> *razed:* destroyed or flattened (such as a building or settlement)

Set a Purpose for Reading: Have students listen to find out what archaeologists learn by uncovering long-buried objects.

During Reading

Use the Think Alouds during the first reading of the selection. Notes about the genre and cultural perspective may be used during subsequent readings.

Search for the Past

from *Dig This! How Archaeologists Uncover Our Past*

by Michael Avi-Yonah

Humans have crafted tools, weapons, clothing, cooking utensils, and many other objects for thousands of years. When these objects broke or wore out, people usually dumped them on a garbage pile and made new things. The discarded objects were often buried under more garbage or under dust, sand, or soil.

In later times, people digging in the ground found some of the objects that were thrown away long ago. The items might be kept out of curiosity. They might be given to a collector of artifacts—objects that are made or modified by humans. This process of discovery and <u>preservation</u> is a simplified example of the science called archaeology.[1] Archaeologists find, collect, study, and preserve artifacts from the past.

The word *archaeology* was first used by the Greeks more than 2,000 years ago. Its first part comes from the Greek word *archaios,* which means "ancient." The second part comes from the Greek word *logos,* which means "speech."

When historians in ancient Greece talked about the past, the discussion was called an "archaeology." Descriptions of the past are now called history, while the study of objects from the past is known as archaeology.

At one time, archaeology was considered a glorified treasure hunt—a search for valuable and interesting objects. In recent times, however, archaeology has developed into a respected scientific <u>field</u>.[2]

The goal of most archaeological expeditions is to explore and explain ancient artifacts in an effort to understand human history. But the focus of archaeology has shifted. For example, instead of asking where and when farming developed, archaeologists now ask how and why prehistoric people began to grow crops.

Few of the objects thrown away thousands of years ago have survived. After 10 or 20 years, most objects had decomposed (broken down) and had mixed with the soil. After 100 years, almost everything had disappeared. The surviving artifacts were made of materials that could withstand harsh climates.

Damp weather quickly destroys cloth, writing paper, and wood. These materials almost never survive, except in the

Think Aloud

[1] *I'm glad the writer defines the words* artifact *and* archaeology. *I think this is important to know because the entire selection is about archaeology.*

Think Aloud

[2] *I find out here that archaeology was not always about learning, but about being the first one to find a treasure. I think knowing this difference is important because now people are much more careful about the treasures they uncover. They also use the artifacts to learn about the cultures that made them.*

deserts where the climate is very dry. Objects made of gold and silver, however, last for hundreds or thousands of years, even when buried in soil. More common metals—such as iron, copper, or bronze—rust or corrode in the ground, but they usually have a better chance of being recovered than valuable gold or silver objects.

Over the centuries, people who found objects made from precious metals often melted them down to make money or jewelry. Pottery and stone objects, on the other hand, are not very valuable and are not easily destroyed. For this reason, almost every archaeological site contains little gold but has large amounts of broken pottery called potsherds.

Without regular repair, even the strongest buildings eventually decayed. Wind and rain quickly destroyed wooden roofs, and earthquakes shattered the strongest stone walls. In addition, people altered buildings and made it difficult for archaeologists to determine when a structure was first inhabited. City dwellers tore down old buildings and put up new ones in the same places. Laborers often used stones and wooden beams from old buildings for new construction.

In ancient times, few cities had garbage collectors, so residents simply threw their trash into the street, where it decayed into the dirt of hard-packed roads. Over time, this gradual <u>accumulation</u> of trash raised the street level so that people walked downstairs to enter their homes. New houses were often built on top of the foundations of old houses. In the new houses, however, the ground floor was level with the street. As a result, the old ground floor lay beneath the new ground floor.

As time passed, streets continued to build up, and the process was repeated. Towns and cities rose higher and higher, forming different levels, or strata, of buried objects. Natural soil processes—such as erosion, weathering, and sedimentation—also help to shape the earth's strata, which accumulate even in modern cities.

Ancient cities, deeply buried tombs, and sunken ships are all places where archaeologists discover past cultures. Some of these archaeological sites were important urban areas that were abandoned or destroyed during a natural disaster or an ancient war. City dwellers who could escape often left their possessions behind. Archaeologists of a later age might find these abandoned belongings.[3]

Modern wars can lead to important archaeological discoveries. During World War II (1939–1945), bombs

Think Aloud

[3] *I wonder what archae-ologists in the future will think about us when they study the possessions we leave behind and the things we throw away.*

<u>razed</u> entire city blocks in London, England. But the terrible destruction left archaeologists with a unique opportunity. A team of researchers dug through the rubble in search of the remains of Londinium, a town built by the Romans around A.D. 43.

The scientists uncovered a temple dedicated to Mithras, a god worshiped by many Roman soldiers. The temple was removed and put on display before new construction covered the site.

Tombs and graves sometimes are the best sources of information about past cultures. Well-preserved bodies can give scientists clues about what people ate and how they died. In many ancient cultures, people buried their dead with charms and valuable possessions, believing the objects would be needed in the afterlife. These artifacts help archaeologists solve the puzzle of how people lived long ago.

Summarize: Remind students that just as an archaeologist carefully brushes away soil from artifacts, a good reader sifts through a nonfiction article for the main idea and supporting details. Ask students to summarize the article.

Student Think Aloud

Use Copying Master number 1 to prompt students to share questions they now have after reading the article.

"I wonder . . ."

Cultural Perspective

Have students research archaeological finds in your own area, using local authorities. Invite a scientist to speak to the class before they do a report about their research.

Think and Respond

1. How can destruction lead to archaeological discovery? What other places are good sources of information for archaeologists? *Possible responses: The bombs that razed London led to the discovery of the remains of Londinium. Tombs and sunken ships are other good sources of information. Well-preserved bodies give clues about what people ate and how they died.* **Analytical**

2. Does the selection present the many facts and details in a way that is easy to understand? Why or why not? *Possible responses: Yes, he explains everything carefully and repeats the main idea. No, he jumps from point to point; it would help if he divided the article into sections with subheadings.* **Genre**

3. What do you think the writer wants us to understand about archaeology? *Possible responses: Archaeology started as a treasure hunt, became a science, and now gives us useful information about people who lived long ago. Archaeology is a challenging process because most artifacts do not survive and those that do are buried deep underground.* **Author's Purpose**

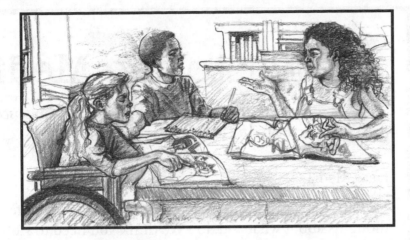

Letter to the Media

by the Sixth Grade Life and Career Skills Class of DeWitt Middle School, Ithaca, NY

Genre: Letter/Critique

Comprehension Strategy: Evaluate

Think-Aloud Copying Master number 4

Before Reading

Genre: Tell students that letters such as the one you are about to read aloud show how many people write open letters to publicly critique something and to persuade others to agree with their opinions and take actions.

Expand Vocabulary: Before reading this letter aloud, explain the following words and terms:

> *open letter:* a published letter meant for everyone to read
>
> *media:* agencies of mass communication, including TV, radio, magazines, newspapers, and the Internet
>
> *runway:* a long platform used by fashion models during a show

Set a Purpose for Reading: Invite students to listen to the letter to find out what motivated a group of middle school students to write a critique of the media.

During Reading

Use the Think Alouds during the first reading of the letter. Notes about the genre and cultural perspective may be used during subsequent readings.

Think Aloud

[1] *The students at this school must have brainstormed and made notes about what they wanted to include in the letter. In this manner, the opinions the letter expresses would belong to the majority and not just to one person.*

Think Aloud

[2] *I figured out that they must be responding to fashion advertisements in magazines because the letter talks about sizes, real faces and bodies, and the editing of pictures. They do not sound very happy with the media about the kinds of images they show.*

Letter to the Media

Students at DeWitt Middle School in Ithaca, NY, composed this open letter to the media and fashion industries.

Dear Media:

Our Sixth Grade Life and Career Skills class has a few thoughts about what you do.[1] We think you need to stop making innocent people feel bad (mainly kids). We believe that you should make more sizes so people won't feel bad about their bodies. Also, stop editing people's pictures so that they look perfect. You need to put people in magazines or articles and use their real faces and bodies, to show that no one is perfect. Showing that everybody has to look a certain way isn't right.

Why are you designing clothes that won't even fit you? The way you design things, you make your models look like stiff dolls. You barely even notice the models walking down the runway. Men should stop making their muscles big by using steroids, because it is disgusting to see all those muscles and veins sticking out of their arms and shirts. It's your fault they're hurting themselves, because of the fake images you show to people.[2] You need to stop worrying about your worthless money.

In all, we want you to stop showing fake images so people won't feel bad about themselves.

Sincerely,
The Sixth Grade Life and Career Skills Class
DeWitt Middle School

Take Notes: Ask students to summarize the objections of the letter writers and how they want the media and the fashion industries to change. Have students write a letter of opinion or persuasion. Tell them to support their opinions with explicit details and use a particular structure for their letter, such as cause/effect or problem/solution.

Student Think Aloud

Use Copying Master number 4 to prompt students to share their understanding of the letter.

"I figured out _____ because . . ."

Think and Respond

1. What do you think the students mean when they talk about everybody having to look a certain way? *Possible response: The students mention the lack of different sizes and an emphasis on perfection in images.* **Inferential**

2. How do you think the students went about creating this letter? *Accept reasonable responses. Possible responses: They probably had a class discussion. Then they brainstormed what they wanted to say. Next, they decided which ideas most students wanted to include. Afterward, they wrote and revised the letter.* **Evaluate**

3. How did this letter influence or change how you view images in the media or fashion industry? *Accept reasonable responses. Possible responses: I agree with the authors' point of view. This letter makes me realize that models do all look the same.* **Author's Purpose**

No Barriers

from *A Special Strength*
by Michael Burgan

Genre: Biography

Comprehension Strategy: Evaluate

Think-Aloud Copying Master number 2

Before Reading

Genre: Inform students that some nonfiction articles tell about a person who overcame a challenge. Explain that they will meet Mark Wellman, a man who became disabled but still reaches new goals in outdoor sports.

Expand Vocabulary: Before reading aloud this nonfiction selection, explain the following words and terms:

> *paraplegic:* a person who cannot move the lower half of his or her body due to a spinal disease or injury

> *positive attitude:* a tendency to focus on good things or ideas

> *depressed:* feeling unhappy or hopeless

> *cross-country:* done over hills or fields, not on roads or a specially prepared area

> *barrier:* something that could stop you from reaching a goal

Set a Purpose for Reading: Ask students to listen for how the author feels about Mark Wellman's achievements.

During Reading

Then use the Think Alouds during the first reading of the selection. Notes about the genre and cultural perspective may be used during subsequent readings.

No Barriers

from *A Special Strength*
by Michael Burgan

Mark Wellman made his way down the mountain. He had just finished climbing the Seven Gables, in California's Sierra Nevadas. Wellman had been climbing mountains since he was twelve. For him, it was as easy as riding a bike or tossing a ball.

Suddenly, Mark's foot slipped on some crumbled rocks. He tumbled down the mountain, falling 100 feet. When he landed, he couldn't move. His back was broken.

On that day in the Sierra Nevadas, Mark Wellman became physically disabled. After the fall, Mark was a <u>paraplegic</u>—he would never be able to use his legs again. Most paraplegics spend their lives in wheelchairs. But Mark was determined to keep climbing mountains and living an active life.[1]

Mark had many battles to fight before he could return to the mountains. First, he had to find a <u>positive attitude</u> again. Mark's injuries <u>depressed</u> him. It was hard for a strong, energetic young man to accept the fact that he'd never walk again. Mark also had to learn new ways to climb and do the other sports he loved. From now on, he'd be able to use the strength only in his arms.

Mark worked hard to get his body in shape. He played tennis while sitting in a wheelchair. He swam for hours in a pool. And he lifted weights to make his arms even stronger than they were before. Finally, Mark was ready for his first major climb since the accident.[2]

In 1989, Mark and his new climbing partner, Mike Corbett, set out to climb the face of El Capitan. El Capitan soars almost 3,000 feet above Yosemite National Park. It's the highest granite rock in the world. El Capitan has a flat surface, like a wall in a room.

Think Aloud

[1]*The writer tells me that Mark is active and skilled, and likes the outdoors. I think Mark may be able to stay active, but I think mountain climbing will be very difficult for him.*

Think Aloud

[2]*I made a connection when I read about what Mark had to do to prepare himself for climbing. I think about how hard it is to do even one chin-up on a bar. I can understand why he had to exercise the way he did. His arms would have to be very strong to move his body weight around.*

Mark became the first paraplegic climber to reach the top of El Capitan.

Mark has kept on climbing since he scaled El Capitan. He's also become active in other sports. Before his accident, Mark was a downhill skier, and he still loves to speed down the slopes. Now, he also skies cross-country. He took part in the 1992 and 1994 Winter Para-Olympics, an event where paraplegics and other physically challenged athletes from around the world compete for medals.

To make cross-country skiing easier, Mark created new equipment for paraplegics. Paraplegic skiers sit on a small seat attached to one ski. Mark improved this design. In 1993, he took his sit-ski on a 50-mile trek across the Sierra Nevadas, skiing trails 10,000 feet high.

Mark has shown that paraplegics can conquer more than mountains—they can ride the waves, too. Inside a kayak (a kind of canoe), Mark rushes down whitewater rivers. For a more leisurely ride, Mark sometimes takes his kayak to the Pacific Ocean. There, he paddles near the whales that play along the California coast.

After Mark Wellman fell that day on the Seven Gables, he could have given up the sports he loves. Instead, he found the inner strength to meet the challenge of his disability. He refused to let his disability become a barrier—something that stopped him from moving forward.

Today, Mark believes people can do anything they want to, if they try hard enough. Mark travels the country, sharing that message with both the physically challenged and the physically able.

The wilderness that Mark loves made him a paraplegic.[3] But he says it gave him something, too: a life full of challenge and joy. Mark adds, "Everyone faces the world with different abilities and disabilities. But everyone has at least one goal in common— to break through their own barriers."

Genre Study

Biography: Writers of biographies about exceptional people often use powerful quotes from that person. A quote is placed at the end of the selection in order to sum up an important message: that all people can achieve their goals if they are determined enough.

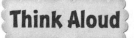

Think Aloud

[3]*The author says that the wilderness was the cause of Mark's disability. I'm not sure I agree with that.*

After Reading

Take Notes: Have students discuss how the author describes the ways that Mark broke through barriers. How does the author feel about Mark's achievements?

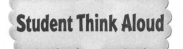

Student Think Aloud

Use Copying Master number 2 to prompt students to relate their feelings and attitudes to those of Mark Wellman.

"I made a connection when..."

Cultural Perspective

In 1984, Neroli Fairhall of New Zealand became the first paraplegic athlete to compete in the Olympics. The competitive archer took up the sport after a motorcycle accident.

Think and Respond

1. Mark says his disability has given him a life full of challenges and joy. How can challenges bring joy to your life? *Possible responses: If I meet a challenge, I am proud of myself. It makes me happy to reach difficult goals.* **Analytical**

2. The writer goes into great detail in his description of El Capitan. Why is it important for readers to know what this rock face is like? *Possible responses: It shows how difficult El Capitan would be for anyone to climb and helps you appreciate Mark's achievement all the more.* **Genre**

3. What do you think the author wants us to learn about ability and disability? *Accept reasonable responses. Possible responses: Everyone faces the world with different abilities and disabilities. People can use their abilities to break through many barriers, even the barrier of disability.* **Author's Purpose**

Sea Talk
by Max Fatchen

Genre: Poem

Poetic Elements: Assonance and Consonance

Comprehension Strategy: Evaluate

Think-Aloud Copying Master number 6

Before Reading

Genre: Explain that a poem can give us a whole new understanding of familiar places. This poem uses rhythm to evoke the sound of the sea and its animals. Point out that the poet also uses assonance and consonance, or the repetition of consonant and vowel sounds.

Expand Vocabulary: Before reading the poem aloud, review the following words with students:

> *harbour:* a body of water near a coast in which ships can anchor
>
> *limpets:* marine animals that have shells and cling to rocks
>
> *pier:* a platform built on stilts that juts out into the water
>
> *murmur:* to make a low or whispering noise
>
> *gossiping:* chatting about everyday events

Set a Purpose for Reading: For the first reading, ask students to listen for assonance, consonance, and rhyme in the poem.

During Reading

For the first reading, use an expressive tone to emphasize the assonance and consonance in the poem. As you read, pause for punctuation to show how the poem imitates the ebb and flow of the tide. In subsequent readings, pause to discuss the Think Aloud and genre note.

Sea Talk

by Max Fatchen

Inside the little harbour, on the tide
That washes stones where weedy limpets cling,
I thought I heard where sleeping rowboats ride,
The little fishes' tiny whispering.

I thought I heard, beside the wooden pier,
The starfish heave a long and salty sigh
And murmur in the mussel's shelly ear,
Its longing for a bright and wider sky.

I thought I heard the underwater shouts
Of gleeful creatures . . . moans and barks and squeals,
The dolphins thrusting long and smiling snouts
And gossiping to sleek and agile seals. . . .[1]

The noises from the restless waves and spray
Of armoured crabs that guard their rocky spots,
The sound of white sea horses at their play
Or lobsters' prayers within their captive pots.

I wish I knew that such a thing could be—
To know the songs of moving fin and scales,
The liquid language of the living sea
And hear the gentle voices of the whales.

Genre Study

Poem: Assonance, or the repetition of vowel sounds, can be found in the words *waves* and *spray*. Consonance, or repetition of consonant sounds, can be found in *sound/ sea horses* and in *murmur/mussel's.*

Think Aloud

[1]*I thought that the descriptions of movement and sound were important to the poet because it's as if the sea and its creatures communicate in their own languages.*

Set a Purpose for Rereading: Reread the poem to discuss the imagery and rhyme in more detail. Point out that the poet also uses personification to give human qualities to the sea animals. Then have students write a response that interprets or critiques the poem with judgments and opinions supported by specific references to the poem.

Student Think Aloud

Use Copying Master number 6 to prompt students to discuss how a detail in the poem changed their understanding of the sea.

"I thought _____ was important in this text because . . ."

Think and Respond

1. What images does the poet use to create the sense of a "liquid language"? *Possible responses: whispering fish; starfish that sigh and murmur; underwater shouts; moans and barks and squeals [of] the dolphins; songs of moving fins and scales; gentle voices of the whales.* **Analytical**

2. What poetic elements are found in "Sea Talk"? Give examples from the poem. *Possible responses: personification, rhythm, imagery, assonance and consonance, rhyme.* **Genre**

3. What does this poem tell you about the poet? *Accept reasonable responses. Possible responses: He enjoys listening to the sea. He has a vivid imagination. He spends a lot of time at the sea.* **Author's Purpose**

Better Than Gold

by Maria Testa

Genre: Realistic Fiction

Comprehension Strategy: Make Inferences and Analyze

Think-Aloud Copying Master number 2

Before Reading

Genre: Tell students that you are going to read aloud a story about two boys who like to run track. Explain that fiction often uses elements of real life. Although Carlos and Bruce are fictional characters, they each deal with situations that can happen in real life. Likewise, other details in the story, such as the setting, will seem familiar to most readers.

Expand Vocabulary: Before reading this story of two sprinters, discuss the following words:

> *100-meter dash:* a track event in which runners compete to run 100 meters in the fastest time

> *Down's syndrome:* a genetic disorder that causes physical and mental disabilities

> *track meet:* a track competition in which participants compete in many events

> *starting blocks:* in track, pads that help runners position their feet at the beginning of a race

Set a Purpose for Reading: Invite students to listen to find out what Carlos learns through his experience. Remind student to make inferences if the information is not stated.

During Reading

Then use the Think Alouds during the first reading of the story. Notes about the genre and cultural perspective may be used during subsequent readings.

Better Than Gold

by Maria Testa

Every time I close my eyes, I see that sidewalk rushing up at me. But that's not the worst of it. The worst part is the wet SNAP!

"Carlos, you have a clean break of the tibia and fibula," Dr. Marino announced.[1] "You'll live, but you won't be running for a while."

Now I'm out for the rest of the track season. I mean, I was everybody's pick. I would have won the city championship in the 100-meter dash. But then, like a complete fool, I ignored Coach Gonzalez's advice.

I went for a run on a city street.

Sure, I was careful to keep an eye out for oncoming traffic. But I didn't count on tripping over a stupid curb.

You should have heard the guys when I showed up at track practice. I was limping on crutches with my left leg in a cast. I wasn't a pretty sight.

"There goes the city championship," Washington moaned.

Coach Gonzalez put an arm around my shoulders. "You know," he said, "you might not be able to run, but you can still make yourself useful."

"What good am I if I can't run?" I asked.

Coach smiled. "This isn't the only team I coach," he said. "And I sure could use your help with my other one. Interested?"

Now, I love track. Just being around people running can lift my spirits.

"Sure," I said. "What do I have to do?"

"Show up here at nine o'clock sharp on Saturday morning. You'll find out then," Coach said mysteriously.

When Mom dropped me off on Saturday, the place was already crowded. Kids were warming up on the track and all over the field. I didn't recognize their team uniforms.

As I crutched along, I noticed that a lot of the kids had Down's syndrome. Some of them were in wheelchairs. In fact, all of them seemed to be kids with special needs. I didn't know what to think.

Coach Gonzalez jogged up to me.

"Good to see you, Carlos!" He clapped me on the back. "Glad you could make it."

"Coach," I blurted out, "I don't know anything about working with these kids!"[2]

"Nothing special to know," he said. "This is a <u>track meet</u>. You know about track meets, don't you?"

"Sure," I said, "but . . ."

"Come with me," Coach interrupted. "I want you to meet someone."

What could I say? I crutched after him.

"Carlos, I want you to meet Bruce. Bruce, this is Carlos." The kid was doing stretching exercises on the grass. He had Down's syndrome.

We stared at each other for a few seconds. Then Bruce jumped to his feet and stuck out his hand.

"How are you doing, Buddy?" he said. "How did you hurt your leg?"

"Ah . . . I was out running, and I tripped on a curb."

Bruce frowned. "You shouldn't run on city streets, Buddy," he said.

Coach Gonzalez laughed. "You tell him, Bruce! Listen, you guys hang out together, OK? Bruce, make Carlos feel at home. Carlos, you help Bruce with his warm-ups. He's a sprinter, too, you know."

"Great!" Bruce said. "Come on, Buddy, you can watch me run." He jogged off to the <u>starting blocks</u>. I looked at Coach Gonzalez.

"What are you waiting for, Carlito? Keep up with him!" he said.

So off I went, crutching furiously after Bruce.

One thing I learned quickly: Bruce could really run. I mean, he definitely knew how to move around a track. As he did his warm-up sprints, he just seemed to get faster. I couldn't wait for his race to begin.

Coach Gonzalez stopped by to check on us. "So how's it going, guys? Having fun?"

I was pretty excited. "Bruce is a great sprinter," I said. "I think we're looking at a *gold* medal here!"

"Well," Coach said, smiling, "Bruce has a different goal this year. Right, Bruce?"

"Right, Coach," Bruce answered.

"OK, guy," Coach said to Bruce. "It's time to hit the starting blocks for real this time."

Bruce held up his hand, and I gave him a high-five.

"Good luck, Bruce," I said. "Go for the **gold**!" He waved and jogged off to the starting line.

"Coach," I said as we headed over to watch the race, "what did you mean when you said that Bruce has a different goal this year?"

"He just wants to finish the race," Coach explained. "Last year, the sound of the starter's gun scared him so much that he never even ran. He just stood at the starting line with his hands over his ears."

"Wow," I whispered. It was hard to imagine, especially since Bruce was such a good runner.

We watched the runners line up. Bruce looked confident as he dropped into his starting position.

"On your mark! Get set!" the starter called. He raised his gun into the air. POW!

The runners were off—all except one.

"Oh, no," Coach said softly. Bruce was standing at the starting line with his eyes shut tight and his hands clamped over his ears.

Without even thinking, I crutched into action.

"Bruce!" I called. I moved awkwardly through the crowd. "Run, Bruce, run! Bruce! Run!" Then I heard Coach Gonzalez's voice.

"Run, Bruce, run!"

The next thing I knew, people all around us were picking up the chant:

"Run, Bruce, run! Run, Bruce, run!"

Bruce opened his eyes. He saw the people clapping and calling his name. Slowly at first, but then gaining speed, he started to run. He sprinted across the finish line—in last place, but with his arms held high over his head. The crowd was cheering wildly. I clapped Coach Gonzalez on the back.

"What do you think?" he asked. "Was it worth it?"

I dropped my crutches and danced on one foot. "It's great," I said. "No, **better** than great. It's **better** than **gold**!"[3]

Genre Study

Fiction: Because this is realistic fiction, success is not measured by a fairy tale ending. Bruce did not win the race. However, Carlos learns an important lesson and Bruce reaches his personal goal.

Think Aloud

[3] *I made a connection at the end of the story. I could see how Bruce and Carlos both changed. Their self-confidence was much greater at the end.*

After Reading

Retell the Story: Have students role play the story. Then have them identify and explain the author's points of view (as first-person narrator and omniscient narrator) and how the voice affects the text.

Student Think Aloud

Use Copying Master number 2 to prompt students to discuss connections they made with characters or events in the story.

"I made a connection when . . ."

Cultural Perspective

Discuss the Special Olympics, specifically what kind of an opportunity this event is for athletes with special needs around the world.

Think and Respond

1. Carlos and Bruce are both male sprinters in track. What else do Carlos and Bruce have in common? *Possible responses: They both have positive attitudes. When Carlos breaks his leg, he is still willing to coach other runners. When Bruce gets scared by the sound of the starting gun, he is willing to go back and try again.* **Critical**

2. What parts of this fictional selection could happen in real life? *Possible responses: People with special needs participate in athletic events. Runners can break legs. The setting, a track meet, can also happen in real life.* **Genre**

3. What does the writer hope readers will learn from this story? *Possible responses: Everybody has their own goals in life. Success means doing your best, not winning championships or coming in first place.* **Author's Purpose**

The Riding Machine

by Barbara Hagen

Genre: Nonfiction Article

Comprehension Strategy: Analyze Text Structure

Think-Aloud Copying Master number 7

Before Reading

Genre: Point out that some nonfiction articles summarize the history of a common item. Inform students that in this article you are about to read aloud, the author tells how the bicycle was invented and explains how it developed into the bike we ride today. Mention that a good writer tries to include only the most important or fascinating details.

Expand Vocabulary: To help students better understand this article, introduce and explain the following words:

cobblestone: streets made long ago using rounded stones

lunge: to suddenly move forward

streamlined: designed something with a smooth shape that moves with minimal resistance through air

Set a Purpose for Reading: Have students listen to find out how bicycles have changed.

During Reading

Then use the Think Alouds during the first reading of the selection. Notes about the genre and cultural perspective may be used during subsequent readings.

The Riding Machine

by Barbara Hagen

People have always wanted to get from one place to another easier and faster. The invention of the wheel in prehistoric times was just the beginning of what would develop from the horse and carriage all the way to the invention of the car and even the airplane. Before the invention of the car, people were experimenting with an idea that would eventually become one of the most popular forms of transportation for kids across America, the bicycle.[1]

In 1817, a man wanted to get around the gardens of his estate faster. He lived in Germany; his name was Baron von Drais. In some ways, his "bicycle" was similar to the bikes of today. It had two same-sized in-line wheels. You could steer the front wheel in the direction you wanted to go. But this all-wooden, two-wheel, *riding machine* had no pedals. Instead you would push your feet against the ground in a sort of glide-walk. This is similar to scooters kids ride today. This vehicle became known as the "draisienne," named for the Baron.

About 40 years later, pedals were added to this *riding machine.* It was called the velocipede or "fast foot." Its nickname was the "boneshaker." Because it was made entirely of wood, *riding* on <u>cobblestone</u> streets would "shake up your bones." In 1871, James Farley invented the high wheeler also known as the "penny farthing." It had a very large front wheel and a small back wheel. The rider sat up very high. Although it became very popular, it was also dangerous. If the front wheel hit a stone or rut in the road or stopped short, the bicycle would <u>lunge</u> forward, and the rider would be dropped on his head. This is where the famous expression "taking a header" comes from.

In the 1880s, a man named H. J. Lawson invented the first bicycle with a chain. It had two wheels the same size and was called the safety bicycle. In 1893, the Wright Brothers, the first men to fly an airplane, opened a bicycle shop selling and repairing bicycles. A lot of the ideas they used in their efforts to fly they got from bicycles.[2]

The next step in the history of bicycles came with the invention of the pneumatic tire. This was a rubber tire filled with air. An Irish veterinarian named Dunlop wanted to make

Think Aloud

[1] *I never considered that the invention of the wheel was just as important to airplanes as it was to cars. Even though the author mentions other types of transportation, I can tell that this article is mostly about bicycles.*

Genre Study

Nonfiction: With each paragraph, the writer gives new information about the bicycle. Because she is describing the history of the bicycle, she starts with its invention and presents her information in time order.

Think Aloud

[2] *I understand now how bicycles relate to airplanes. This shows how one invention can lead to others. I wonder which parts of bicycles helped the Wright Brothers with their invention.*

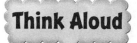

a more comfortable bike for his son. Dunlop is a successful tire company today.

Early in the 20th century, most of the attention on transportation turned toward the car. But after World War I, interest in bicycles became popular again as manufacturers began making a heavy bike that copied designs of airplanes and rockets. The "kid bike" was on every child's wish list.[3] By the 1960s they were becoming more streamlined. The three speeds of the 1960s grew to 10 speeds in the 1970s.

Today mountain bikes with bigger tires have become popular again. Many people like to go *riding* on mountain trails. Bicycle racing is also popular with the success of an American, Lance Armstrong, who overcame cancer to win the Tour de France, the most important bicycle race in the world.

Think Aloud

[3] I can see why bikes designed like airplanes and rockets would be on every child's wish list. If I lived back then, I would want one of these bikes, too!

Take Notes: Work with students to create a time line. Discuss what information is most important to include, such as the date, a brief description of the bicycle or how it was changed, and the name of each person who helped make that change.

Student Think Aloud

Ask students to summarize a section from the article. Use Copying Master number 7 to prompt students to discuss how the details support the main idea and the article as a whole.

"This is mostly about . . ."

Cultural Perspective

Bicycles have inspired people to come up with new ideas, freeing people from the horse and carriage and leading the way for the car and airplane. In the 1890s, bicycle riding also freed women's style of dress, putting an end to bustles, corsets, and other articles of clothing that restricted movement.

Think and Respond

1. How do today's bicycles compare with early bicycles, such as the draisienne and the penny farthing? *Possible responses: The newer ones have pedals and chains, are safer and more streamlined, and can go faster. Unlike today's bicycles, the draisienne was made of wood. The penny farthing had two wheels of different size and the rider sat up very high.* **Analytical**

2. In order, list the ways the bicycle has changed since 1817. *Possible responses: The first bike was wooden and had no pedals. A later bike had a large front wheel. Bikes came to look more like the models we have today.* **Genre**

3. Why did the author write about the history of this invention? *Accept reasonable responses. Possible responses: Perhaps she wanted readers to know how long the bicycle has been around and how much it has changed. Maybe the author is a bicyclist and wants to share her interest with others.* **Author's Purpose**

The Sayings of Confucius

by Confucius

Genre: Nonfiction (Primary Source)
Comprehension Strategy: Evaluate
Think-Aloud Copying Master number 4

Before Reading

Genre: Tell students that the nonfiction selection you are going to read is a collection of thoughtful quotations said by one person long ago. Such statements are also called *sayings*. Remind students that throughout history and around the world, many men and women have been great thinkers. This selection is based upon the writings of Confucius, a wise teacher who lived almost three thousand years ago in China.

Expand Vocabulary: Before reading aloud the sayings of Confucius, discuss the following words and terms with students:

> *obligated:* to have a duty or responsibility
>
> *unrighteous:* acting without honor or kindness
>
> *nature:* the character or essence of someone or something
>
> *inferior:* not as good as, or less than, someone or something else

Set a Purpose for Reading: Encourage students to listen to evaluate whether what Confucius said long ago is still helpful today.

During Reading

Use the Think Alouds during the first reading of this selection. Notes about the cultural perspective may be used during subsequent readings.

The Sayings of Confucius

by Confucius

For thousands of years China has been shaped by the values of family loyalty and hard work. A major influence on Chinese civilization has been Confucius (kun FYOO shus), a philosopher and teacher born in 551 B.C. In the hope of preventing wars, Confucius taught that kindness and respect in the family form the foundation of a peaceful society. Confucius stressed that rulers are also <u>obligated</u> to be honest and just. The passages below are some of Confucius's teachings that his students later wrote down. How do the teachings of Confucius still relate to life today?

Having only coarse food to eat, plain water to drink, and a bent arm for a pillow, one can still find happiness therein. Riches and honor acquired by <u>unrighteous</u> means are to me as drifting clouds.[1]

Those who know the truth are not up to those who love it; those who love the truth are not up to those who delight in it.

By <u>nature</u> men are pretty much alike; it is learning and practice that set them apart.

Shall I teach you what knowledge is? When you know a thing, say that you know it; when you do not know a thing, admit that you do not know it. That is knowledge.

Tzu Kung asked: "Is there any one word that can serve as a principle for the conduct of life?" Confucius said: "Perhaps the word 'reciprocity': Do not do to others what you would not want others to do to you."[2]

The gentleman first practices what he preaches and then preaches what he practices.

The gentleman understands what is right; the <u>inferior</u> man understands what is profitable.

Think Aloud

[1] *I figured out what this means because after I thought about it, it sounded familiar. It means that money does not buy happiness!*

Think Aloud

[2] *I wonder what the word* reciprocity *means. The next part says that you should treat people the way you want to be treated. So reciprocity must have to do with giving and taking in equal amounts.*

爸 爸 媽 咪 榮 譽 和 平

愛 福 德

The gentleman makes demands on himself; the inferior man makes demands on others.[3]

A government is good when those near are happy and those far off are attracted.

~~~~~~

After Confucius died in 479 B.C., his teachings were handed down by others. His ideas about respect and honesty became part of the fabric of Chinese society and spread across Southeast Asia. His teachings remain a major influence throughout much of Asia and the world.

Take Notes: Invite students to listen carefully for key words, such as *learning, happiness,* and *truth,* as you slowly reread each saying. Ask students to make notes of these words to come up with a list of qualities that Confucius valued most. Have students evaluate whether these qualities are still valued today. Help students recognize that their own point of view contributes to their ability to form an opinion.

Student Think Aloud

Use Copying Master number 4 to prompt students to analyze one of the sayings in the text.

"I figured out _____ because _____ ."

Cultural Perspective

About a century after Confucius's time, a book called the *Tao Te Ching,* or "The Way of Virtue," also became widely read. Some people say that this book, rather than being written by the author, Lao Tzu, which means "wise teacher," was actually the work of several people.

Think and Respond

1. In what ways is the wisdom of Confucius still helpful to us today? *Possible responses: Some things, like truth and kindness, never change. Many of these are familiar sayings today, such as "Do unto others as you would have them do to you." These are rules for behavior that are fair and considerate, which never go out of style.* **Critical**

2. The editor lists the sayings one after another without giving explanations. Why do you think he did this? *Possible responses: Perhaps he felt that Confucius's wisdom was the most important thing for people to remember about him. Perhaps the editor wanted people to think through these ideas on their own and apply them to their own lives. By including only sayings, it was easier for people to study and remember them.* **Genre**

3. Why do you think the students of Confucius handed down his teachings? How would things be different if they had not? *Possible responses: They wanted everyone to learn from his wisdom. Asian culture and that of other parts of the world would not have been influenced by the wisdom of Confucius.* **Author's Purpose**

JUMP START:

AN AFTER-SCHOOL PROGRAM KIDS LEAP AT
by Scott Ingram

Genre: Nonfiction Article

Compehension Strategy: Evaluate

Think-Aloud Copying Master number 5

Before Reading

Genre: Tell students that the informational text you are about to read aloud tells about a volunteer program for kids. Point out that a good nonfiction writer always gives the complete name of the program or organization, explains what the purpose of the group is, and then usually gives some examples of how the program works.

Expand Vocabulary: To help students appreciate this article, explain the following words and expressions:

> *same old same old:* a boring routine
>
> *well-structured:* designed to be clear and orderly
>
> *geared to:* designed for
>
> *sibling:* a brother or sister
>
> *benefits:* helps

Set a Purpose for Reading: Tell students to listen to evaluate the author's purpose for writing this article.

During Reading

Use the Think Alouds during the first reading of the selection. Notes about the genre and cultural perspective may be used during subsequent readings.

JUMP START:
AN AFTER-SCHOOL PROGRAM KIDS LEAP AT

by Scott Ingram

What are you doing after school? Text messaging the friends you just saw in school? Doing your usual mouse potato routine—killing time in front of the computer? Checking out what's in the fridge, maybe inhaling last night's leftovers?[1] Let's face it: Late afternoon is a dead zone in the day for many kids.

But not Keyanna Fields. She has figured out how to escape the same old same old. Keyanna, 11, was playing at a gym with some friends, coming up with rhymes jazzy enough to jump rope to. The girls had just finished reading about a kid who used her jump rope skills to meet others when she moved to a new neighborhood. Keyanna and her friends were laughing and tripping over the spinning rope, trying to recite their rhymes in time to jump.

Keyanna lives in New Haven, Conn., and belongs to an after-school program that keeps her happy and busy four afternoons a week. The program is called LEAP, which stands for Leadership, Education, and Athletics in Partnership. Since 1992, when the program was founded, LEAP has turned empty afternoons into well-structured, fun hours for more than 10,000 young people in Connecticut.

LEAPs AND BOUNDS

LEAP is geared to young people ages 7 through 12. LEAP matches the kids with counselors who are in high school or college. From Monday through Thursday, 3:30 P.M. to 6:00 P.M., each counselor serves as part teacher, part big sibling, and part good friend to the younger kids.

Keyanna isn't the only satisfied LEAPer. Dominique Warner, 11, counts herself among LEAP's many fans. Dominique said she likes the program for a simple reason: "I know where I'm going to be every day."

A typical LEAP day for Dominique begins when she gets off the school bus. Soon after, her LEAP counselor, Barbara King, 19, arrives from her college classes. Then King, Dominique,

Think Aloud

[1]At first I was puzzled by the phrase "inhaling last night's leftovers." Then I found out the author is exaggerating reality by using hyperbole, or added emphasis, to catch my attention.

and several other seventh-grade girls walk to the Conte/West Hill School that acts as their meeting place. LEAPers meet at several different locations around the city. High school student Shantelle Brooks, 16, who works with King, hands out apples for the daily snack. Then everyone gets busy with homework. Boys and girls work in separate groups.

ACADEMICS, ATHLETICS, AND ATTENTION

Ask any LEAPer and he or she will agree that LEAP is definitely about reading. Shared reading—where kids read aloud and discuss stories—is a daily activity.

In a second-floor science lab of the Conte/West Hill School, some sixth- and seventh-grade boys work with their counselor, Tayshaun Bell. Bell, 19, is a college basketball player who wants to become a crime scene investigator.[2] Like many counselors, Bell was once a LEAPer. Bell takes out the book that the boys have been reading—*Hoops*, by well-known author Walter Dean Myers—and begins to read aloud.

Meanwhile, a group of fourth- and fifth-grade boys meet with their counselor, Jeremy Black, 17, at a round table in one corner of the school cafeteria. LEAP suggests that no more than four kids work with each counselor so that a counselor can give everyone close attention. When Black notices that Freddie Jimenez, 10, is having trouble with math word problems, the counselor pulls up a chair next to the fifth-grader to help. "Let's try it this way," Black, an honor student, says as he patiently helps Freddie read the word problems until the fifth-grader understands.

At the end of each day, kids and counselors join in a sharing circle and talk about good things they "picked up" that day. They also talk about bad things they "left behind." Then the groups walk together to their homes. Counselors make sure an adult is present at every LEAPer's home.

COMMUNITY EFFORT

LEAP owes its success to people who understand that working together <u>benefits</u> everyone in a community. One proof of the program's success is that teachers report that LEAP students have better school attendance and cause fewer problems than other kids of the same age.

Think Aloud

[2] *I don't need to remember the name of each person and school in this article. I know that these details are included to help me understand that this article is about real people and places.*

Genre Study

Nonfiction Article: Nonfiction articles provide readers with enough information to fully understand the topic. The writer of this nonfiction article explains in detail how the program works day to day.

More than 90 percent of LEAP kids read at grade level or above. More than 90 percent of LEAP's junior counselors graduate from high school. And more than 85 percent of LEAP counselors go on to college. Those percentages are almost twice as high as those of New Haven kids who do not participate in LEAP.

LEAP is so popular that there are more interested kids than available spots. For many kids, LEAP afternoons have a way of becoming LEAP years.[3] Some of the teens who are counselors now were once kids who participated in the program. "I've worked at LEAP for four years, and I was a LEAP kid before that," says King. "LEAP is a big part of my life."

An A-Plus Plan for Success

Barnetta Haywood, 18, has had the chance to be with LEAP for several years as a LEAP kid and a counselor. A high school senior, she plans to go on to college and hopes for a career in law enforcement. LEAP has made a big difference in her life. "I'm naturally shy and quiet," Haywood says. "LEAP has helped me come out of my shell. Working with my group of girls forces me to talk a lot. It's good for me."

LEAPers learn about the program through their school and in the community. Admission is on a first-come basis, so kids have to jump on it.

Set a Purpose for Rereading: Have students evaluate what LEAP stands for, what it does, and whether it is successful or not. Then ask students how the author feels about LEAP.

Student Think Aloud

Use Copying Master number 5 to prompt students to think aloud about their understanding of the article.

"I noticed the author used . . ."

Cultural Perspective

Another volunteer organization for young people is the Boys and Girls Club of America. It gives children a safe place to learn and grow all over the United States, including seventy-seven American Indian, native Hawaiian, and native Alaskan communities.

Think and Respond

1. What do you think life would be like for students if they did not have the LEAP program? What kind of experiences would they miss? *Possible responses: Perhaps many children would not have anything to do after school. They might do poorly in school because they have no one to help with their homework. Some children may not have older siblings. This program gives children role models.* **Analytical**

2. Why do you think the writer includes quotations from a few students who have taken part in the program as well as other details about them? *Possible responses: It helps readers understand what it might be like to be in the program. Having different people give facts and opinions about the program brings the article to life and makes it more interesting.* **Genre**

3. Why do you think the author wrote about this after-school program? *Possible responses: to show that programs like this help young people succeed; to draw attention to the needs of students after regular school hours; to show that many teenagers volunteer to help younger students* **Author's Purpose**

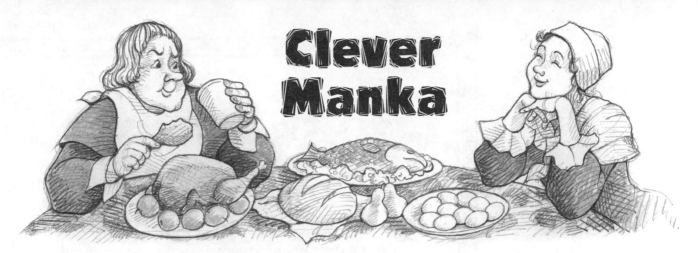

Clever Manka

a folk tale from Czechoslovakia
retold by Parker Fillmore

Genre: Folk Tale

Comprehension Strategy: Analyze Story Structure

Think-Aloud Copying Master number 5

Before Reading

Genre: Before reading aloud this folk tale about a clever young woman named Manka, remind students that folk tales are stories that have been told and retold for many generations. Inform students that this is a realistic folk tale because, even though it is make-believe, some of the events could really happen. The main character, Manka, uses her wits to answer riddles and solve problems.

Expand Vocabulary: Before reading this Czechoslovakian folk tale, discuss the following words:

> *unscrupulous:* acting without concern for fairness or honesty
>
> *proposal:* a suggestion or plan
>
> *pompous:* having an exaggerated sense of self-importance
>
> *interfering:* becoming involved in other people's business; getting in the way

Set a Purpose for Reading: Invite students to listen to this folk tale to find out how Manka uses her cleverness to solve problems and to right wrongs.

During Reading

Use the Think Alouds during the first reading of the story. Notes about the genre and cultural perspective may be used during subsequent readings.

Clever Manka

a folk tale from Czechoslovakia
retold by Parker Fillmore

There was once a rich farmer who was as grasping and unscrupulous as he was rich. He was always driving a hard bargain and always getting the better of his poor neighbors. One of these neighbors was a humble shepherd who, in return for service, was to receive from the farmer a heifer. When the time of payment came, the farmer refused to give the shepherd the heifer, and the shepherd was forced to lay the matter before the burgomaster.

This burgomaster, who was a young man and as yet not very experienced, listened to both sides, and when he had deliberated, he said: "Instead of deciding this case, I will put a riddle to you both, and the man who makes the best answer shall have the heifer. Are you agreed?"

The farmer and the shepherd accepted this proposal and the burgomaster said: "Well, then, here is my riddle: What is the swiftest thing in the world? What is the sweetest thing? What is the richest?[1] Think out your answers and bring them to me at this same hour tomorrow."

The farmer went home in a temper.

"What kind of burgomaster is this young fellow!" he growled. "If he had let me keep the heifer, I'd have sent him a bushel of pears. But now I'm in a fair way of losing the heifer, for I can't think of any answer to his foolish riddle."

"What is the matter, husband?" his wife asked.

"It's that new burgomaster. The old one would have given me the heifer without any argument, but this young man thinks to decide the case by asking us riddles."

When he told his wife what the riddle was, she cheered him greatly by telling him that she knew the answers at once.

"Why, husband," said she, "our gray mare must be the swiftest thing in the world. You know yourself nothing ever passes us on the road. As for the sweetest, did you ever taste honey any sweeter than ours? And I'm sure there's nothing richer than our chest of golden ducats that we've been laying by these forty years."

The farmer was delighted.

"You're right, wife, you're right! That heifer remains ours!"

Think Aloud

[1]When I read the riddle for the first time, I had to reread it to make sure that I thoroughly understood it. Now that I comprehend the riddle, I am also interested in thinking about the solution and wondering how the riddle will be solved.

The shepherd, when he got home, was downcast and sad. He had a daughter, a clever girl named Manka, who met him at the door of his cottage and asked: "What is it, father? What did the burgomaster say?"

The shepherd sighed.

"I'm afraid I've lost the heifer. The burgomaster set us a riddle, and I know I shall never guess it."

"Perhaps I can help you," Manka said. "What is it?"

The shepherd gave her the riddle, and the next day, as he was setting out for the burgomaster's, Manka told him what answers to make.

When he reached the burgomaster's house, the farmer was already there rubbing his hands and beaming with self-importance.

The burgomaster again propounded the riddle and then asked the farmer his answers.

The farmer cleared his throat and with a <u>pompous</u> air began: "The swiftest thing in the world? Why, my dear sir, that's my gray mare, of course, for no other horse ever passes us on the road. The sweetest? Honey from my beehives, to be sure. The richest? What can be richer than my chest of golden ducats!"

And the farmer squared his shoulders and smiled triumphantly.

"H'm," said the young burgomaster dryly. Then he asked: "What answers does the shepherd make?"

The shepherd bowed politely and said: "The swiftest thing in the world is thought, for thought can run any distance in the twinkling of an eye. The sweetest thing of all is sleep, for when a man is tired and sad, what can be sweeter? The richest thing is the earth, for out of the earth come all the riches of the world."[2]

"Good!" the burgomaster cried. "Good! The heifer goes to the shepherd!"

Later the burgomaster said to the shepherd: "Tell me now, who gave you those answers? I'm sure they never came out of your own head."

At first the shepherd tried not to tell, but when the burgomaster pressed him, he confessed that they came from his daughter, Manka. The burgomaster, who thought he would like to make another test of Manka's cleverness, sent for ten eggs. He gave them to the shepherd and said: "Take these eggs to Manka and tell her to have them hatched out by tomorrow and to bring me the chicks."

Think Aloud

[2] To understand just how clever Manka is, I can compare the shepherd's answer to the farmer's answer by rereading both answers. From the answers, I can see that the farmer is selfish while Manka is very thoughtful.

When the shepherd reached home and gave Manka the burgomaster's message, Manka laughed and said: "Take a handful of millet and go right back to the burgomaster. Say to him: 'My daughter sends you this millet. She says that if you plant it, grow it, and have it harvested by tomorrow, she'll bring you the ten chicks and you can feed them the ripe grain.' "

When the burgomaster heard this, he laughed heartily.

"That's a clever girl of yours," he told the shepherd. "If she's as comely as she is clever, I think I'd like to marry her. Tell her to come to see me, but she must come neither by day nor by night, neither riding nor walking, neither dressed nor undressed."

When Manka received this message, she waited until the next dawn when night was gone and day not yet arrived. Then she wrapped herself in a fish net and, throwing one leg over a goat's back and keeping one foot on the ground, she went to the burgomaster's house.

Now I ask you: did she go dressed? No, she wasn't dressed. A fish net isn't clothing. Did she go undressed? Of course not, for wasn't she covered with a fish net? Did she walk to the burgomaster's? No, she didn't walk, for she went with one leg thrown over a goat. Then did she ride? Of course she didn't ride, for wasn't she walking on one foot?

When she reached the burgomaster's house, she called out: "Here I am, Mr. Burgomaster, and I've come neither by day nor by night, neither riding nor walking, neither dressed nor undressed."

The young burgomaster was so delighted with Manka's cleverness and so pleased with her comely looks that he proposed to her at once and in a short time married her.

"But understand, my dear Manka," he said, "you are not to use that cleverness of yours at my expense. I won't have you interfering in any of my cases. In fact, if ever you give advice to anyone who comes to me for judgment, I'll turn you out of my house at once and send you home to your father."

All went well for a time. Manka busied herself in her housekeeping and was careful not to interfere in any of the burgomaster's cases.

Then one day two farmers came to the burgomaster to have a dispute settled. One of the farmers owned a mare that had foaled in the marketplace. The colt had run under the wagon of the other farmer, and thereupon the owner of the wagon claimed the colt as his property.

The burgomaster, who was thinking of something else while the case was being presented, said carelessly: "The man who found the colt under his wagon is, of course, the owner of the colt."

As the owner of the mare was leaving the burgomaster's house, he met Manka and stopped to tell her about the case. Manka was ashamed of her husband for making so foolish a decision, and she said to the farmer: "Come back this afternoon with a fishing net and stretch it across the dusty road. When the burgomaster sees you, he will come out and ask you what you are doing. Say to him that you're catching fish. When he asks you how you can expect to catch fish in a dusty road, tell him it's just as easy for you to catch fish in a dusty road as it is for a wagon to foal. Then he'll see the injustice of his decision and have the colt returned to you. But remember one thing: you mustn't let him find out that it was I who told you to do this."

That afternoon, when the burgomaster chanced to look out the window, he saw a man stretching a fish net across the dusty road. He went out to him and asked: "What are you doing?"

"Fishing."

"Fishing in a dusty road? Are you daft?"

"Well," the man said, "it's just as easy for me to catch a fish in a dusty road as it is for a wagon to foal."

Then the burgomaster recognized the man as the owner of the mare, and he had to confess that what he said was true.

"Of course the colt belongs to your mare and must be returned to you. But tell me," he said, "who put you up to this? You didn't think of it yourself."

The farmer tried not to tell, but the burgomaster questioned him until he found out that Manka was at the bottom of it. This made him very angry. He went into the house and called his wife.

"Manka," he said, "did you forget what I told you would happen if you went interfering in any of my cases? Home you go this very day. I don't care to hear any excuses. The matter is settled. You may take with you the one thing you like best in my house, for I won't have people saying that I treated you shabbily."

Manka made no outcry.

"Very well, my dear husband, I shall do as you say: I shall go home to my father's cottage and take with me the one thing I like best in your house.[3] But don't make me go until after supper. We have been very happy together and I should like to eat one last meal with you. Let us have no more words but be kind to each other as we've always been and then part as friends."

Think Aloud

[3] I notice that the author often has characters repeat lines. I think the author does this for emphasis. For example, the burgomaser tells Manka to take what she likes best. In her response, Manka echoes the burgomaster by saying she will take the thing she likes best. I have a feeling this is the key to Manka's solution.

The burgomaster agreed to this, and Manka prepared a fine supper of all the dishes of which her husband was particularly fond. The burgomaster opened his choicest wine and pledged Manka's health. Then he set to, and the supper was so good that he ate and ate and ate. And the more he ate, the more he drank until at last he grew drowsy and fell sound asleep in his chair. Then without awakening him, Manka had him carried out to the wagon that was waiting to take her home to her father.

The next morning, when the burgomaster opened his eyes, he found himself lying in the shepherd's cottage.

"What does this mean?" he roared out.

"Nothing, dear husband, nothing!" Manka said. "You know you told me I might take with me the one thing I liked best in your house, so of course I took you! That's all."

For a moment the burgomaster rubbed his eyes in amazement. Then he laughed loud and heartily to think how Manka had outwitted him.

"Manka," he said, "you're too clever for me. Come on, my dear, let's go home."

So, they climbed back into the wagon and drove home.

The burgomaster never again scolded his wife, but thereafter whenever a very difficult case came up, he always said: "I think we had better consult my wife. You know she's a very clever woman."

Retell the Story: Invite students to retell their favorite episode in the story. Then, have students extend the selection by creating alternate endings, new dialogue between Manka and her husband, or presenting a new riddle.

Student Think Aloud

Use Copying Master number 5 to prompt students to recall one of the scenes in detail.

"I noticed the author used . . ."

Cultural Perspective

Folk tales in which a clever (or not so clever) character must solve a riddle appear in many cultures, including European, African, native Hawaiian, and Asian cultures. Compare the themes, conflicts, and figurative language from other stories.

Think and Respond

1. Although this is a single folk tale, it has many episodes or parts. Which episode do you think does the best job of showing how clever Manka is? Why? *Responses will vary. Possible response: I think the final episode where Manka takes her husband shows how clever she is. I can tell that she solved this problem right away because she was not immediately upset about her husband's decision to make her leave.* **Inferential**

2. How can you tell that this is a folk tale? *Possible response: It is an old story that has been told many times. It features a clever character who outwits others.* **Genre**

3. Why do you think people have told and retold this folk tale for so many generations? *Possible responses: It reminds them of everyday problems and real people. It is humorous and entertaining. It pokes fun at powerful people and shows ordinary people at their best.* **Author's Purpose**

MONEY: IT'S A NECESSITY

From *Ultimate Kids' Money Book*

by Neale S. Godfrey

Genre: Nonfiction

Comprehension Strategy: Evaluate

Think-Aloud Copying Master number 6

 Before Reading

Genre: Inform students that some nonfiction, like the excerpt you are about to read aloud, takes a closer look at common objects. This excerpt investigates something people use every day—money. Point out that because the topic is so broad, the writer will include facts that have to do with many times and places. Remind students that most nonfiction gives answers to questions such as *what, who, when, where, why,* and *how.*

Expand Vocabulary: Before reading aloud this selection, explain the following terms:

> *distinct:* clearly different

> *minted:* turned metal into coins

> *scarcity:* a very limited amount; not enough of something

Set a Purpose for Reading: Ask students to listen to evaluate and determine if the text is informational or persuasive.

During Reading

Use the Think Alouds during the first reading of the selection. Notes about the genre and cultural perspective may be used during subsequent readings.

MONEY: IT'S A NECESSITY
by Neale S. Godfrey

Can you imagine life without money? How would you pay for food, clothing, and shelter? Could you go to the movies? Could you buy a CD?[1] Without money, you probably wouldn't survive very well!

Money isn't everything. A lot of great things are free. You don't need money to see a full moon or a colorful sunrise. You don't need money to have friends. You don't even need money to have fun! But in today's world, you need enough money to get by, to satisfy some of your needs.

You need money to buy goods, such as food and clothing. You need money to pay for a place to live or to travel on a bus or a train. You need money to pay for services provided by doctors and dentists.

Think about it. You need money for just about everything.

THE FIRST COINS

No one knows for sure who the first people were to use coins. Some people think it was the Sumerians, an ancient people who lived in Mesopotamia (which is now part of Iraq and part of Syria) about 5,000 years ago. Others believe it was the people of Egypt, around 2500 B.C.[2] These people melted and shaped silver into tiny bars. Each was then stamped with its weight and used as money.

By 700 B.C., each Greek city had its own <u>distinct</u> flat pieces of metal that were stamped with a picture or a design. These were the first true coins to be <u>minted</u>. By 500 B.C., coins were being used as money all over Greece and Rome.

GOLD!

In 640 B.C., Lydia, an ancient kingdom in what is Turkey today, used electrum to make its coins. Electrum is a natural mixture of gold and silver that is often found in rivers. To honor the king of Lydia, the coins were stamped with a lion's head.

Think Aloud

[1]*The passage begins with a lot of questions. I think these questions are important because they help me think about how money affects my daily life. The questions also prepare me for the facts that will be presented in the story.*

Think Aloud

[2]*Money is such an important part of my life. I can see why ancient peoples would also need a monetary system to help them in their daily lives.*

Genre Study

Nonfiction: Good nonfiction writers do not only report one fact after another. As this article shows, they use the facts to tell interesting true stories about the topic.

Think Aloud

[3] I was surprised when the writer included information about Robin Hood. But then I saw that he did so to help explain why people stopped carrying gold coins and began carrying paper money instead.

Lydia was the first country to use gold in its money. Gold coins eventually became the most valuable of all metal money.

Because pure gold is very soft, it is often mixed with other metals to make it harder. This mixture is called an alloy. The amount of gold in an alloy is measured in karats. One karat is ¹⁄₂₄ of the alloy.

Gold keeps its value because of its <u>scarcity</u>. There are estimated to be about 95 tons of gold in the world. That much gold would create a cube that measured 19 yards on each side!

EUREKA!

About 2,000 years ago, the Chinese invented both paper and a printing process. They also invented paper money! China did not have a large enough supply of metals for making coins. Instead, they hit upon the idea of making money out of paper. Each paper note was guaranteed by the government to have a certain value. Paper money quickly became their medium of exchange!

Europe at that time was using only coins. So when the explorer Marco Polo returned to Italy from China in 1295, he brought back exciting news: China had been using paper money for hundreds of years! But Europeans couldn't understand how paper could be valuable. It took another 400 years before Europeans caught on and started making paper money of their own.

GUARD YOUR GOLD!

By the time of the Middle Ages in Europe (A.D. 800–1100), gold had become a popular medium for trade. But gold was heavy and difficult to carry. As only kings had access to safes, people often carried all their money around with them. That was a particular problem for wealthy people. Besides, streets and roads were not safe. It was dangerous to carry large amounts of gold.

The legend of Robin Hood began and spread quickly in the Middle Ages. He and his followers lived in the forest, stealing gold from the rich to give to the poor. To prevent people from having to carry so much gold, merchants and goldsmiths started issuing notes, promising to pay gold to the person carrying the note. These promissory notes were the beginning of paper money in Europe.[3]

BEFORE ITS TIME

Still, people in Europe felt safer using coins. Gold and silver were precious metals that would never lose their value because they could always be melted down. In the Middle Ages, Europe was made up of many small states that were at constant war with one another. The people did not have enough confidence in their governments to trust paper money. In fact, it wasn't until 1661 that Sweden became the first European country to print money on paper.

After Reading

Take Notes: Help students create a two-column chart to compare and contrast coins and paper money. Have students use their charts to summarize how money was first invented and how paper money came to replace gold.

Student Think Aloud

Use Copying Master number 6 to prompt students to think aloud about what they learned as they read this selection.

"I thought _____ was important in this text because . . ."

Think and Respond

1. This article explains how money has changed over the centuries. How does money continue to change in our world? *Responses will vary. Possible responses: Money has changed with new technology, such as bank cards and the Internet. Money can now include checks, debit cards, and credit cards.* **Analytical**

2. The writer includes many dates, names of places, and other details. Discuss how this helps to make the text more believable and reliable. *Possible response: If an author uses dates, locations, and events in an article, this allows the reader the opportunity to look up these facts to make sure the article is true and accurate.* **Genre**

3. What does the author want to teach you about money? *Possible responses: You need money for most things. People started using coins thousands of years ago. Gold is the most valuable metal because it is scarce. For a long time, people felt safer using coins rather than paper money.* **Author's Purpose**

Rock Hound

by Kristin Baird Rattini

Genre: Informational Nonfiction (Primary and Secondary Sources)

Comprehension Strategy: Analyze Text Structure

Think-Aloud Copying Master number 4

Before Reading

Genre: Point out that some informational texts are articles. Many articles also include interviews. Explain that an interview is a report based on questions a reporter asks another person. In the article you are about to read aloud, point out that the reporter interviewed a man who has been a rock collector for more than ten years. The interview includes details about his particular collection as well as advice for other people who are interested in rock collecting.

Expand Vocabulary: To help students better understand this selection, introduce the following words:

> *geologist:* a scientist who studies the structure of Earth and its rocks
>
> *rock hound:* somebody who is enthusiastic about collecting rocks and minerals
>
> *Smithsonian:* a museum located in Washington, D.C.; encompasses several different museums, including one for geologic collections
>
> *deplete:* take away; decrease

Set a Purpose for Reading: Have students listen to find out why Russell, the subject of this interview, likes to collect rocks and what his collection includes.

During Reading

Use the Think Alouds during the first reading of the selection. Notes about the genre and cultural perspective may be used during subsequent readings.

ROCK HOUND

by Kristin Baird Rattini

The Eagle Scout from Spencerville, Ind., has traveled from Ohio to Idaho in search of rare and cool rocks for his impressive collection.

"I like the uniqueness of each rock," says Russell, 20. "No two pieces are alike."

The son of a <u>geologist</u>, Russell became a true <u>rock hound</u> himself at age 9, after a family rock-collecting trip out West.[1]

HEY, IT'S YOUR COLLECTION

From the few pieces of agate that Russell found on that trip, his rock collection has grown to more than 150 items. He also shares in his dad's collection of more than 1,000 pieces.

Some rock hounds collect rocks for their beauty. Others choose them for their rarity. Russell's collection is a little bit of both.

"You collect what interests you," he says. "If something looks neat but is not worthy of the <u>Smithsonian</u>, it doesn't mean you can't have it."

Among his many finds, Russell has two favorites: copper from Michigan's Upper Peninsula and blue celenite he found in an Ohio mine.

"I stepped around a large rock, and the celenite was lying on the ground there by chance," he says. "It was a beautiful find."

PATIENCE IS A VIRTUE

It's rarely that easy to find rocks that are keepers. Rock hounds often must use hammers, chisels and picks to pry rocks out of the ground. And just because someone struck gold in a spot yesterday doesn't mean you'll find anything there today.

"You have to be very patient," Russell says. "There's no guarantee you'll find anything of significance, so it takes some dedication."

For every rock he collects, Russell writes down the date, location and type of rock. He usually can name the rock by sight using rock identification guides.

Think Aloud

[1] I figured out why Russell likes to collect rocks. He sees the uniqueness in each one. Also, his dad is a geologist and the family goes on rock-collecting trips. No wonder he is a rock hound.

Genre Study

Nonfiction: Using interview notes, the writer presents a primary source, or firsthand information by reporting word-for-word what the person said. Information the author read and used to develop the story would be considered secondary sources.

If he's stumped, Russell might ask his rock club for help. He and his father belong to three; he considers club members his mentors. "A club gets you involved with people who really know the ropes for your area," Russell says. "There's always someone who knows the answer to your questions."

JOIN THE CLUB

A rock club is the best place for new collectors to learn about the hobby, Russell says. Besides advice, clubs often give new members an egg carton full of rock samples to help start their collections.

Then newbies are ready to join the hunt![2] Rocks are everywhere, from your backyard and schoolyard to local fields and forests. You also can shop at local rock and mineral shows to add more variety to your collection. "Buying enables you to add pieces you'd never get to dig up yourself," Russell says.

As your collection grows, you'll need a system to organize it. Some people use tackle boxes; others use buckets. Egg cartons also are popular.

Although they've been around for thousands of years, rocks can be fragile. Handle carefully, cleaning them with only mild soap and water, if necessary.

RESPECT AND REWARDS

Not all collectors treat rocks and the environment with respect. Some tear up property as they dig. Others deplete an area of its supply, ruining the site for everyone else.

As a result, rock collecting has become more difficult in recent years. Some sites once open to rock hounds are now off limits (as are all national and most state park sites).

Despite these obstacles, rock collecting can be a fun and rewarding hobby.

"One of the greatest things about rock collecting is that you're part of the life span of that mineral," Russell says. "Since the time that rock was created, you could be the first human being to see it. It's electrifying."

Think Aloud

[2]*I can figure out that* newbies *are beginners, or people who are new at something. The previous paragraph talks about new collectors and new members. Then, the author uses the word* newbies. *This must be a slang term for a person new at something.*

DIG IT!

Eagle Scout Russell Greim says it's easy to start collecting rocks, Anyone can do it with this short list of supplies:

- Rock identification guide (Many types are available at libraries, bookstores and on the World Wide Web.)
- Safety glasses
- Rock hammer
- Small plastic bags (for your rock specimens)
- Paper and pen (to catalog your finds)[3]

Once you've collected your supplies, you're ready to collect some rocks. Remember, safety is a top priority:

- Wear a hard hat. It's usually required when digging in mines.
- Use the buddy system.
- Be aware of your surroundings. Look out for overhangs and loose boulders.
- Always ask for permission before digging on private land.

Think Aloud

[3] *I notice the author uses a list to tell what supplies I would need and safety tips I should remember. This is easier to listen to and understand because the list items are generally short and simple. If the items were in long sentences and paragraphs, I might not remember the items so easily.*

Take Notes: Ask students to summarize the article and discuss how well the topic was addressed and how the ideas were organized. Then have students think of a topic and list examples of primary and secondary sources to investigate the topic. Instruct them to develop and discuss criteria for evaluating sources for credibility and reliability. Guide students to consider timelines, author's background, accuracy of information, and any author bias that might affect the credibility of the story.

Student Think Aloud

Use Copying Master number 4 to prompt students to discuss discoveries they made about rock collecting.

"I figured out _____ because _____."

Cultural Perspective

The world is full of rock hounds or rock collectors. Some collectors are interested in many types of rocks, while some collectors are only interested in one type of rock. The world's biggest rock is Uluru, also known as Ayer's Rock, in Australia. Made from a single piece of sandstone, this rock is sacred to the Aboriginal people.

Think and Respond

1. What are the differences between primary and secondary sources and how does having a primary source affect the reliability and accuracy of the informaton presented? *Possible responses: Primary sources are firsthand information sources such as interview or autobiography. Secondary sources are information sources that are evaluations and interpretations of primary sources after the fact. Having a primary source in your writing can help make the writing more credible and accurate.* **Critical**

2. How can you tell that this article is based on an interview? How would the article be different if the writer had not taken the time to meet a real rock hound? *Possible responses: This article is based on an interview because the writer presents some information by directly quoting what someone said about rock collecting. The article would not be as interesting or as personal because Russell's comments help the reader understand the experience of rock collecting instead of only learning facts about it.* **Text Structure**

3. How might this selection inspire someone to become a rock hound? *Possible responses: The author includes a list of things a beginning rock collector would need. The author shows what rock collecting is really like and how interesting it could be.* **Author's Purpose**

Words Do Not Pay

by Chief Joseph

Genre: Nonfiction Speech

Comprehension Strategy: Evaluate

Think-Aloud Copying Master number 2

Before Reading

Genre: Tell students that the selection you are going to read aloud is a speech, a talk given to many people at once. In 1879 Chief Joseph, a Nez Perce Indian, gave this speech in Washington, D.C., to emphasize that people's actions must live up to their words. Chief Joseph defended the rights of all Americans, including his people. Explain that the speech uses repetition to get its message across. It also has a turning point, a part when the speech shifts direction by introducing a new idea.

Expand Vocabulary: Before you read aloud the speech, explain the following words and phrases:

> *misrepresentation:* deliberately false account of something

> *penalty:* legal punishment, such as a fine or imprisonment

> *eloquence:* expressive or persuasive language

> *fell on deaf ears:* people did not listen

Set a Purpose for Reading: Ask students to listen to the tone, mood, and emotions of Chief Joseph's words.

During Reading

Use the Think Alouds during the first reading of the speech. Notes about the genre and cultural perspective may be used during subsequent readings.

Words Do Not Pay

by Chief Joseph

I do not understand why nothing is done for my people. I have heard talk and talk, but nothing is done. Good words do not last long unless they amount to something. Words do not pay for my dead people. They do not pay for my country, now overrun by white men. They do not protect my father's grave. They do not pay for all my horses and cattle. Good words will not give me back my children. Good words will not make good the promise of your war chief General Miles. Good words will not give my people good health and stop them from dying. Good words will not get my people a home where they can live in peace and take care of themselves.[1] I am tired of talk that comes to nothing. It makes my heart sick when I remember all the good words and all the broken promises. There has been too much talking by men who had no right to talk. Too many misrepresentations have been made, too many misunderstandings have come up between the white men about the Indians. If the white man wants to live in peace with the Indian he can live in peace. There need be no trouble. Treat all men alike. Give them all the same law. Give them all an even chance to live and grow.[2] All men were made by the same Great Spirit Chief. They are all brothers. The earth is the mother of all people, and all people should have equal rights upon it. You might as well expect the rivers to run backward as that any man who was born a free man should be contented when penned up and denied liberty to go where he pleases. . . .

Let me be a free man—free to travel, free to stop, free to work, free to trade where I choose, free to choose my own teachers, free to follow the religion of my fathers, free to think and talk and act for myself—and I will obey every law, or submit to the penalty.

Chief Joseph
NEZ PERCÉ *Tsutpeli*

Chief Joseph's eloquence fell on deaf ears. He never saw his homeland again.

Think Aloud

[1] *I notice that Chief Joseph uses some of the same words again and again. He wants readers to question whether "good words" are enough to help Chief Joseph and his people. I think his purpose is to embarrass the listener or make them sympathetic, so the listener will take action.*

Think Aloud

[2] *I made a connection when Chief Joseph called for justice and the call for justice in the Declaration of Independence. Both texts have some of the same themes—that all people should be equal.*

Genre Study

Speech: Sometimes a speech points out examples of injustice or other problems. It then declares how to make things right.

Take Notes: Have students discuss the emotions of the speech. Ask students how the emotions are tied to persuasion and persuasive language.

Student Think Aloud

Use Copying Master number 2 to prompt students to share their responses to the speech.

"I made a connection when . . ."

Cultural Perspective

Missonaries were among the first wave of Euro-American settlers to arrive in Nez Perce territory around 1834. The missionaries were very successful at persuading their fellow Euro-Americans to settle on Nez Perce land. By the 1860s and 1870s, the colonizers had broken many of the government treaties and forced many native peoples on to reservations. Chief Joseph's people tried to escape this imprisonment by fleeing to Canada. They were stopped only 50 miles from the border by the U.S. military and sent to a reservation.

Think and Respond

1. How does this speech show that "actions speak louder than words"? Which point does Chief Joseph make that you feel is most important? *Possible responses: People have used "good words" to make promises that have never come true. Chief Joseph wants to see things happen, not just hear people talk about them. The most important point he makes is when he says to treat all men alike.* **Critical**

2. To make readers feel sympathy for his people and their situation, what does Chief Joseph do? *Possible responses: He describes how his people are either dead or in poor health, they are without their homes, and all the things they have lost. He also describes how the government has mistreated and lied to him.* **Genre**

3. What is Chief Joseph's perspective? How does this drive his purpose in writing? *Possible response: Chief Joseph is in a desperate situation and his frustration drives him to speak out against the injustice committed against him.* **Author's Purpose**

At the Medici Villa

written and compiled by the Virtual Renaissance Team

Genre: Dramatic Monologue

Comprehension Strategy: Generate Questions

Think-Aloud Copying Master number 4

Before Reading

Genre: Point out that some narrative selections present history in a dramatic monologue, a speech by one character that tells a story. In this monologue, a son of the Medicis, a powerful family in Italy during the Renaissance, tells readers the true life story of the artist Michelangelo. Mention that the monologue invites readers to imagine something impossible—meeting someone who knew Michelangelo personally. When something impossible in literature seems real, it is called suspension of belief.

Expand Vocabulary: To help students better understand this selection, introduce the following words and phrases:

> *aristocratic:* royal
>
> *dignity:* a sense of pride and self-respect
>
> *manual laborers:* people whose work is mostly physical
>
> *fancied himself:* thought of himself
>
> *melancholy:* sad, depressed

Set a Purpose for Reading: Have students listen to analyze the monologue as a source of information about culture.

During Reading

Use the Think Alouds during the first reading of the selection. Notes about the genre and cultural perspective may be used during subsequent readings.

Genre Study

Dramatic Monologue: A dramatic monologue can be a creative way to present real facts about another time and place. This monologue brings history to life by letting the readers imagine meeting someone who can tell about his or her personal experiences with an event, a place, or a person.

Think Aloud

[1] *I can figure out what the narrator means by the father's "main preoccupation" because that's just another way of saying that something was on his mind a lot. His top priority was to make life better for his family again.*

At the Medici Villa

written and compiled by
the Virtual Renaissance Team

I am a son of Lorenzo De' Medici. Welcome to my villa outside of Rome. I have been told by my servants that you wish to speak to me of Michelangelo Buonarroti. I will give you as much information as I remember. My father started a school for young sculptors in Florence, Italy, in 1489, and Michelangelo attended.

I learned later that he was born on March 6, 1475, in Caprese, Italy. This is a small town about forty miles from Florence. His father was Lodovico di Leonardo Buonarroti Simoni, the magistrate of the town and his mother was Francesca di Neri. The family was an old one with aristocratic beginnings, but they fell on hard times in the middle of the 15th century. It therefore became the father's main preoccupation to restore the family to its former glory.[1] The family returned to Florence when Michelangelo was only a month old. His father sent him immediately to the family farm at nearby Settignano to be looked after by a wet-nurse and her family, stonecutters by trade.

His mother was not well and died when Michelangelo was only six. When he was ten, his father called him to Florence to live there with him and his new wife. It was then that Michelangelo attended school for the first time, four years later than most children. Michelangelo did not take to his lessons well, preferring to spend his time with the young apprentices from the artists' workshops in the city. This angered his father, as an artistic career was thought beneath the dignity of a member of his family. This was because painters and sculptors were considered manual laborers at this time. His father finally gave in to Michelangelo's passion for art and apprenticed him at the age of 13 to a leading Florentine painter, Domenico Ghirlandaio, who taught him how to paint in fresco.

A year later, Michelangelo left to join my father's school where he far outshone the other pupils. One other pupil at the time was Pietro Torrigiano who was filled with jealousy over Michelangelo's talent and picked a fight with him one day. Unfortunately, Michelangelo's nose was broken in the fight and always left him with the feeling that he was ugly thereafter.

My father made up for this incident though, as Michelangelo was so talented. My father brought him to live in the Medici palace in Florence. He participated in the lessons with me and my brothers and sisters and in discussions with the leading scholars and poets who visited my house. He began to write down his thoughts in poetry, a practice he continued throughout his life.

When my father died in 1492, Michelangelo moved back to his father's house and then fled to Venice during the political unrest at the time. He didn't return to Florence until 1495.

Five years later, in his mid-twenties, he established his fame with a breathtakingly beautiful sculpture for St. Peter's church in Rome. It was called the *Pieta*. By now it was he that was supporting his father and four brothers.

His next ambitious project was the sculpture of *David*, more than 12 feet high, in 1504.[2] Now his fame grew and he took on far more work than he could actually complete. This frustrated and saddened him as he expected perfection from himself in his work. He became increasingly absorbed in his work and took little care of his appearance. He even had trouble keeping servants because of the squalor in which he lived. He slept in his clothes and barely took time to eat, satisfying his hunger with a piece of bread.

By 1505, Michelangelo's main patrons were a succession of popes. This resulted in his being given some marvelous opportunities, like the decoration of the Sistine ceiling by Pope Julius II in 1508. I believe his old apprentice still works there. He felt great pressure from his patrons. I remember him saying once, "I cannot live under pressures from patrons, let alone paint." [*quoted in Vasari's* Lives of the Artists]

A few years after completing the Sistine ceiling, Michelangelo returned to Florence where he worked for two Medici popes for over 14 years, but he settled permanently in Rome in 1534. He had a small but close circle of friends and a special relationship with a woman, Vittoria Colonna. Vittoria lived in a convent but often went to Rome to visit Michelangelo where they discussed poetry and religion. It was a terrible blow to Michelangelo when she died in 1547.

Even though Michelangelo fancied himself a sculptor more than anything else, his work in his later years was in fresco painting and architecture. At the age of 66, he completed a huge fresco called "The Last Judgement" for above the altar at the Sistine Chapel.

Think Aloud

[2] *I wonder who David was. I wonder if David was a sculpture of a real person or just the name given to the statue by the artist. Since this is based on real facts about Michelangelo, I can research the details later to find out more information about this artwork.*

At 71, he took over the rebuilding of St. Peter's as the church architect. He went riding in the countryside on a cold rainy day in February, 1564 and returned home to become ill with a fever. Six days later, on February 18, 1564, Michelangelo was dead.

Ah, all this talk has made me <u>melancholy</u>. You should stop by the Sistine Chapel and seek out Michelangelo's old apprentice. Ask him about Michelangelo's work with the Sistine Chapel.[3] Here, I will give you a letter of introduction.

Think Aloud

[3] *As I read this, I have forgotten if the Sistine Chapel is in Rome or Florence. I can reread to check for the correct information, and I notice that he returned to Florence after painting the Sistine ceiling, so the chapel must be in Rome.*

Take Notes: Invite students to summarize Michelangelo's life. Discuss what information is most important to include.

Student Think Aloud

Use Copying Master number 4 to prompt students to encourage them to restate selected paragraphs in their own words.

"I figured out _____ because _____."

Cultural Perspective

Michelangelo lived during the Renaissance, which occurred in the early fourteenth to late sixteenth centuries. The word *renaissance* is French for "rebirth." During the Renaissance, there was a widespread rebirth of interest in the art and wisdom of ancient cultures.

Think and Respond

1. What kind of pressure do you think Michelangelo experienced from his patrons, or those who supported his work with money? *Possible responses: They might have wanted him to work quickly. They might have wanted him to paint certain things in a certain way.* **Analytical**

2. This dramatic monologue gives a personal look at the life of Michelangelo. What phrases does the author use to indicate the passage of time? How does the author tie these sequence phrases into the story? *Possible responses: when he was ten, four years later, at the time, when my father died in 1492, his next ambitious project, a few years after completing the Sistine ceiling; includes precise details in these phrases that relate directly to the story, such as the year his father died, the age of Michelangelo, and the names of the artist's projects.* **Genre**

3. The Virtual Renaissance Team gives important information about Michelangelo by having readers imagine that they are visiting the home of someone who knew him. Why do you think they chose this type of selection? How did the creation of this character and this monologue affect the work? *Possible responses: It makes it easier for readers to understand that Michelangelo was a real person with a childhood, a family, and friends. It brings history to life.* **Author's Purpose**

Limericks

Genre: Limerick

Poetic Elements: Rhyme and Rhythmic Patterns

Comprehension Strategy: Generate Questions

Think Aloud Copying Master number 7

Before Reading

Genre: Explain that a limerick is a poem with a specific rhyme pattern. The first, second, and fifth lines rhyme, and the third and fourth lines rhyme. A limerick has a galloping rhythmic pattern that is very distinctive. Tell students that the three limericks you are going to read aloud are examples of poems that are written primarily to entertain, and do not always make logical sense.

Expand Vocabulary: Before reading the limericks aloud, review the following words with students:

> *infinite:* unlimited or never-ending
>
> *slime:* watery mud or other unpleasant sticky liquid
>
> *faster than light; relative:* a reference to Einstein's theory of relativity, his explanation for the relationship of time, space, energy, and matter
>
> *previous:* occurring before

Set a Purpose for Reading: Ask students to listen to enjoy the fun and humor of each limerick.

During Reading

For the first reading, use a lighthearted tone and read without interruptions. As you read, emphasize the lilting rhythm, regular rhyme pattern, and the punch line at the end of each limerick. Between subsequent readings, pause to discuss the Think Aloud and genre note.

Limericks

A scientist living at Staines
Is searching with infinite pains
    For a new type of sound
    Which he hopes, when it's found,
Will travel much faster than planes.

R. J. P. Hewison

A luckless time-traveler from Lynn
Leaned too close for a look and fell in
    To a puddle of slime
    On the first day of time
And so, naturally, couldn't have been.

X. J. Kennedy

There was a young lady named Bright,
Who traveled much faster than light.
    She started one day
    In a relative way,
And returned on the previous night.[1]

A. H. Reginald Buller

Genre Study

Limericks: Limericks are entertaining verses written in definite patterns of rhyme, *aabba,* and with a lilting rhythm. The length and rhythm of the third and fourth lines are different from those of the remaining lines, giving limericks their distinctive pattern of rhythm.

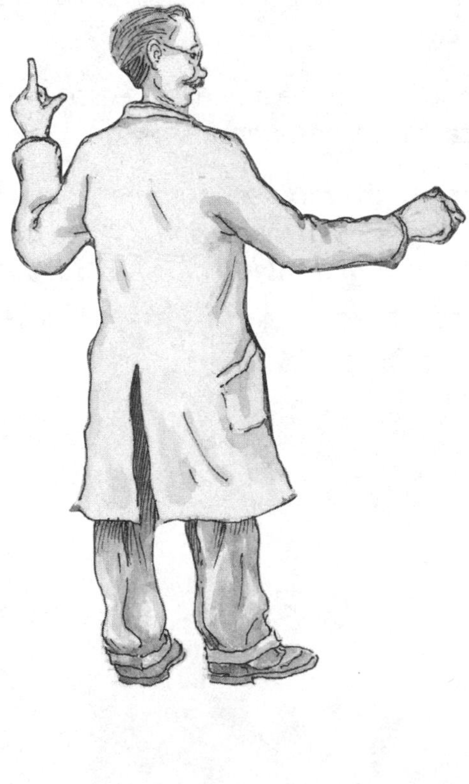

Think Aloud

[1] *I just noticed something about these limericks. They are mostly about science. I guess that poetry can sometimes have fun with serious topics!*

Set a Purpose for Rereading: Reread the limericks to discuss the rhyme and rhythm in more detail. Invite students to clap along with the rhythm and then challenge them to re-create the rhythm from memory. Encourage students to write limericks of their own with the same plot.

Student Think Aloud

Use Copying Master number 7 to prompt students to summarize the humorous story each limerick tells.

"This was mostly about . . ."

Cultural Perspective

Nobody is sure just when and where limericks began. However, poets in County Limerick, Ireland, were writing them as early as the eighteenth century.

Think and Respond

1. How are these limericks serious and also just plain fun? Which limerick is your favorite? Why? *Responses will vary. Encourage students to give reasons for their opinions and to cite a specific detail in the poem. Possible responses: They use scientific ideas, such as the speed of sound and light, to tell nonsense stories for entertainment.* **Analytical/Critical**

2. What poetic elements do you find in all three limericks? *Possible responses: rhyme and rhythm patterns; alliteration; consonance.* **Genre**

3. Why do you think that even some of the most serious poets write limericks? *Possible responses: for the fun of playing with rhyme and rhythm; to make readers laugh; to create something imaginative and entertaining* **Author's Purpose**

The Touch of Sense

by John Kitching

Genre: Poem

Poetic Elements: Imagery

Comprehension Strategy: Summarize

Think Aloud copying master number 3

Before Reading

Genre: Remind students that a poem can use imagery to help readers imagine something they see and feel everyday. This poem uses imagery to remind us of all that we can experience through our sense of touch. Point out that some of the imagery also "touches on" our sense of hearing.

Expand Vocabulary: Before reading the poem aloud, review the following words with students:

> *sense:* the physical way people get information, including sight, hearing, feeling, smell, and touch

> *warts:* harmless bumps that can form on the body

> *mysteries:* things that are difficult to understand or explain

Set a Purpose for Reading: For the first reading, ask students to listen for enjoyment. Have them close their eyes and picture each image the poet describes.

During Reading

For the first reading, read without interruption, pausing at the end of each line to allow students to picture the imagery of fingers. As you read, emphasize words such as *steely, silkenwood,* and *ivoried,* which add to the poem's tactile quality. For subsequent readings, pause to discuss the comprehension Think Aloud and genre note.

Genre Study

Poem: The poet's imagery of fingers ends by showing readers that fingers also write words. The image reminds readers to use their sense of imagination as well as their physical senses.

Think Aloud

[1] *I have never heard the word* silkenwood. *Yet I am able to picture in my mind a polished wooden guitar and to imagine how it might feel to touch it. Although it is made of wood, its smooth surface would feel silky to the touch.*

The Touch of Sense

by John Kitching

Fingers make for miracles

Despite time's <u>warts</u> and hairs.

They smoothe tired children's heads

They ease our daily cares.

They pluck the steely strings

Of silkenwood guitars.[1]

They punch the richest meaning

From ivoried piano keys.

Fingers carve new tales

From long-dead stones and trees.

They plant, they reap,

They hold, they wisely heal.

And fingers give long life

To <u>mysteries</u> of words.

Set a Purpose for Rereading: Reread the poem to discuss the imagery in more detail. Ask students to draw conclusions about the style, mood, and meaning of the poem, based on the poet's word choices. Invite students to write their own poems, using figurative language that appeals to one or more senses.

Student Think Aloud

Use Copying Master number 3 to prompt students to describe one of the lines in more detail.

"I was able to picture in my mind . . ."

Cultural Perspective

Many people of long ago produced stone images to represent their religion, legends, and culture. The Olmecs, an ancient civilization of Mexico, were skilled carvers of stone heads, some as tall as 10 feet and weighing 20 tons.

Think and Respond

1. What images does the poet create to show what fingers are like? Identify some. *Possible responses: They are marked by time. They can comfort and care for someone. They can make music and art, make things that outlast themselves, grow the food that keeps us alive, heal people who are sick or hurt, and record words.* **Inferential**

2. What are some of the senses that the imagery makes you think of? *Encourage students to identify one or more of the five senses and to relate it to a line in the poem. Possible response: The line "they pluck the steely strings" may remind a student of the sense of touch (the feel of plucking thin, metal strings), sound (details about the kind of music they hear), and sight (the musicians they picture playing the instruments).* **Genre**

3. What do you think the poet wants us to remember as we read this poem? *Possible responses: Our fingers are not something to take for granted. Our different senses are connected to each other. Fingers can do many creative and helpful things.* **Author's Purpose**

The People, Who Were They?

from *Stories on Stone*
Rock Art: Images from the Ancient Ones
by Jennifer Owings Dewey

Genre: Autobiography

Comprehension Strategy: Generate Questions

Think-Aloud Copying Master number 3

Before Reading

Genre: Inform students that sometimes a nonfiction article, such as the one you are about to read, uses the writer's own personal experiences to explore a larger topic. Explain that this selection tells about rock art in the American Southwest. The writer includes both personal memories of looking at rock art and descriptions about rock art itself. Mention that in addition to sharing information, nonfiction writers may also share questions they might have about a topic.

Expand Vocabulary: Before reading aloud this selection, discuss the following words:

> *boulders:* large, round rocks
>
> *figures:* human shapes; individuals who are not clearly seen
>
> *traces:* signs that something or somebody was once present
>
> *remote:* hard to reach; far from people and cities

Set a Purpose for Reading: Ask students to listen to find out the historical and cultural aspects found in the narrative.

During Reading

Use the Think Alouds during the first reading of the selection. Notes about the genre and cultural perspective may be used during subsequent readings.

The People, Who Were They?

from *Stories on Stone*
Rock Art: Images from the Ancient Ones

by Jennifer Owings Dewey

When I was a child, growing up in the Southwest, my family took car trips. We often went in search of rock art—ancient images on stone that are found throughout the region.

One hot July day, my parents, brother, and I walked single file along a ridge in the Mimbres Valley, a rock art site in southern New Mexico. The stone under our feet was volcanic— black <u>boulders</u> tumbled on a steep slope.[1] Pecked into the rock surfaces were hundreds, if not thousands, of images. There were pictures of birds, snakes, deer, mountain sheep, and suns.

Some of the <u>figures</u> were eight feet tall. Others were six feet high, or three. Some measured only inches. To my eyes, each one was magical and strange.

A picture of a turtle caught my eye. I tried to imagine the person who had created it. I had been reading and studying all I could about rock art. And although little is known of the people who chipped out the rock images in the Mimbres Valley, since they left few <u>traces</u> of their lives behind, I knew enough to help my imagination along.

I knew that the turtle's creator might have lived in the valley two thousand years before my visit there. I decided the artist was a man—thin, with long black hair hanging loose. I pictured him pecking at the black volcanic rock with a hard stone, one he had used again and again.

I imagined the man was a husband and father, with a wife and children waiting for him in a grove of cottonwoods not far off.[2] There, too, would be the other members of his clan. Many clans—bands of people who lived and traveled together—took their names from animals. Perhaps this clan had named itself after the turtle.

I imagined that the man was making the turtle to thank the spirits—for good luck in hunting—or perhaps to ask for better luck in the next hunt.

Once finished with his work, the man would rejoin his family and clan members in the trees. He would know that anyone passing would see the turtle and understand what it meant.

Think Aloud

[1] *I notice the author gives details that would help me find this place on a map.*

Think Aloud

[2] *I can picture in my mind the ancient rock artist making a picture of a turtle on the dark rock with a sharp stone, just as the writer imagined it. I can also picture his family waiting for him in the grove of trees.*

On another family trip, we visited Nine Mile Canyon, a <u>remote</u> rock art site in southern Utah. We hiked deep into the canyon, where I saw images painted on sandstone walls. Some of the pictures were of kachinas, spirits that are half human, half god. The kachina figures were ten feet tall, with boxy bodies and shields. Their faces were covered by masks decorated with zigzags and circles.

I also saw painted images of antelope, bird tracks, and mountain sheep, as well as handprints—many of which fit my own ten-year-old hands.[3] Later I learned that handprints are universal. They exist on walls and stone all around the world.

Rock art occurs wherever people once lived or camped. These marks on stone say, "We were here. We traveled this way." These pictures are a mysterious but readable record of human history.

Take Notes: Have students use the Internet to look at rock art in the Southwest. Then have them write an opinion or judgment about the ideas and themes presented. Was the language precise or vague?

Student Think Aloud

Use Copying Master number 3 to prompt students to recall images they visualized in their own minds.

"I was able to picture in my mind . . ."

Cultural Perspective

In the Hopi language, *ka* (kuh) means "respected" and *china* (CHEE-nuh) means "spirit," so a kachina is a respected spirit.

Think and Respond

1. What did you find out about the rock art of the Southwest? Why does the writer think they were created in the first place? *Possible responses: They are ancient images in stone. Some of the pictures are of animals, kachinas, and handprints. Some pictures were only a few inches high, while others were several feet high. The artists made the pictures by chipping into the rock with a sharp stone. The writer thinks some of the pictures were to thank the spirits or ask for luck, and to leave proof that the artists were there.* **Analytical**

2. At one point the writer describes herself, her brother, and her parents as figures who are walking single file along a ridge. Why do you think she included this? *Possible responses: She wanted to create an image in words that is like an image of figures on the rocks. Perhaps she wanted to compare her family to that of the rock artist.* **Genre**

3. Why do you think the writer wrote about rock art in such a personal way? *Possible responses: Maybe she wanted to show that her childhood experiences led to a lifelong interest in rock art. She wanted to help readers understand the connection between the art and the artists.* **Author's Purpose**

Volcano!

by Stephen James O'Meara

Genre: Informational Nonfiction

Comprehension Strategy: Summarize

Think-Aloud Copying Master number 5

Before Reading

Genre: Tell students that some nonfiction selections report in depth on a subject. Explain that the author of the selection you are about to read aloud describes volcanoes from a global perspective, comparing and contrasting those found around the world. Mention that it is important to evaluate sources of information based on the publication date, coverage, points of view, and sources. It is a good resource that can be read and referenced again and again.

Expand Vocabulary: Before reading about volcanoes, discuss the following words and phrases with students:

> *molten:* changed into liquid by heat
>
> *pent-up energy:* a power that is held in and builds up force
>
> *potential hazards:* possible dangers; usually dangers that can be prevented
>
> *friction:* the resistance between two things when they rub together

Set a Purpose for Reading: Tell students to listen to find out why scientists study volcanoes and how volcanoes differ around the world.

During Reading

Use the Think Alouds during the first reading of this selection. Notes about the genre and cultural perspective may be used during subsequent readings.

Volcano!

by Stephen James O'Meara

Genre Study

Nonfiction: In this in-depth nonfiction article, the writer gives detailed explanations and examples. These examples reinforce the ideas the author presents.

As you read this sentence chances are that <u>molten</u> rock is bleeding from Italy's Mount Etna in Sicily, volcanic bombs are exploding out of Arenal volcano in Costa Rica, and lava rivers are pouring from Hawaii's Kilauea volcano. Volcanologists, the men and women who study these living mountains, expect such behavior. In fact, right now about 10 volcanoes are erupting somewhere on Earth. It's a natural way for our planet to release <u>pent-up energy</u>.

Earth is dappled with volcanoes—perhaps more than 40,000. About 1,300 are potentially active (meaning they've erupted in the last 10,000 years), and most lie beneath the world's oceans. It's the volcanologists' job to monitor these "windows" to Earth's interior. Their biggest challenges: to predict when a volcano will erupt, to educate local officials about <u>potential hazards</u>, and to set up early warning systems. These measures can save (and have saved) many lives.

All Volcanoes Are Not Alike

Like people, each volcano looks and behaves differently. Some, like conical Mount St. Helens in Washington state, blow gas and ash high into the atmosphere. Others, like long and smooth Kilauea, gush molten lava. And those like Arenal and Etna shoot out mixtures of both. Generally, a volcano's location and composition reveal a lot about how it works.[1]

The Earth's crust is broken into a dozen sections, called tectonic plates, that fit together like a jigsaw puzzle. Some sections move as much as 8 inches per year, and most volcanic activity occurs along their boundaries. If two plates separate, fluid volcanoes fill the gap. The islands of Iceland and the Mid-Atlantic Ridge are examples of this. They belong to a submarine volcanic ridge that runs down the middle of the Atlantic Ocean.

The famous Ring of Fire—the world's largest volcanic "necklace"—marks where the Pacific Ocean's floor plunges underneath the continents surrounding it. The <u>friction</u> between the rubbing plates there melts rock and dissolves seawater, creating a gaseous magma that rises and explodes to the surface as a volcano. The violent eruption of Mount Pinatubo in the Philippines occurred along the Ring of Fire.

Think Aloud

[1] *This paragraph is important because it describes the causes and effects of different types of volcanoes. I enjoy learning information like this.*

The fluid lava that flows across the island of Hawaii, however, might originate in the Earth's liquid outer core. Large teardrops of molten rock rise through the mantle and puncture the crust at points called "hot spots." In the case of Hawaii, that event happened in the middle of the Pacific plate, at ocean bottom. The island of Hawaii's Mauna Loa, the world's largest volcano, rises 31,000 feet above the ocean floor—about 2,000 feet higher than Mount Everest. That's a lot of lava!

Because they rarely explode, the Hawaiian volcanoes of Mauna Loa and Kilauea are relatively safe to watch, even up close. Imagine standing near a molten river at night, watching a vent spray lava 1,000 feet skyward. The volcano sounds like a low-flying 747 jet, and the heat is so intense that your skin tingles. You dare not venture closer. Beside you, a lava flow snaps, crackles, and pops—like a bowl of Rice Krispies in milk.

On the other hand, nothing in nature can match the power of the volcanoes that dot the Ring of Fire. Two out of every three of Earth's land volcanoes are there, and Indonesia alone harbors more than 127 of them. Some are furious. For example, in 1815, Tambora, near Bali, exploded with the energy of 800,000 hydrogen bombs! It poured about 170 billion tons of volcanic debris into the atmosphere, caused 12,000 deaths on the island, and created a giant sea wave that killed another 80,000 people on two neighboring islands. By comparison, the energy released by Mount St. Helens in 1980 was equal to 400 hydrogen bombs and volcanic debris claimed 57 lives.

The Good Side of Volcanoes

Volcanoes may cause death, but they also sustain life. Ash, for example, is rich in soil nutrients important to plant growth. The livelihood of many developing countries, therefore, depends on agricultural products grown in the fertile soils that surround volcanoes.[2]

The gases making up Earth's early atmosphere were expelled by volcanoes. Today, emissions from Mount Etna alone make up 10 percent of all the carbon dioxide gas that the Earth releases. Etna might also have caused climate changes during the past 10,000 years.

Volcanic ash and gases do affect climate. Tambora caused the "year without a summer." El Chichon apparently provoked a severe Northern Hemisphere winter in 1984. And the Earth's average global temperature dropped 1.5 degrees Fahrenheit because of Mount Pinatubo's eruption in 1991. That drop was enough to offset the slight temperature increase Earth was experiencing around that time, which some scientists attributed to global warming.[3]

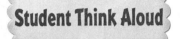

After Reading

Take Notes: Ask students to list as many facts about volcanoes as they recall from the selection. Then reread the article, and have students determine the appropriateness and accuracy of the author's facts and conclusions.

Student Think Aloud

Use Copying Master number 5 to prompt students to share details they noticed from the selection and how the author presented them.

"I noticed the author . . ."

Cultural Perspective

In Hawaiian, *Kilauea* means "much spreading" or "spewing," and *Mauna Loa* means "long mountain."

Think and Respond

1. What was the most surprising fact you discovered about volcanoes? *Encourage students to locate details in the text to make their answers as specific as possible. Possible response: Volcanoes can be helpful and not just harmful.* **Analytical**

2. Do you think that the writer made a good choice by including so much detail about so many different volcanoes? Why or why not? *Accept reasonable answers. Possible responses: Yes, it helped me learn as much as possible about volcanoes. Yes, if I forget any important details I can reread the article. No, it would have been easier to follow if he just told about one volcano in detail.* **Genre**

3. Why do you think the author wrote this article? *Possible responses: Perhaps he wanted to tell readers that there is more to volcanoes than they may realize. He wanted to show how volcanoes affect the world around us.* **Author's Purpose**

Plays

RECYCLING:
Taming the Plastic Monster!
by L. E. McCullough

Basic Concept:

This play introduces recycling—specifically the theory and process of recycling plastic—and explores related topics of pollution, landfills, toxins and the impact of recycling on the environment.

Pre- or Post-Play Activities:

- Have students go on a scavenger hunt around the school to find an example of each plastic type.

- Have students make posters detailing the seven categories of recycled plastic.

- Have students think of which common plastic materials might be used as bird houses and bird feeders—then make some!

- Have a contest for the most original art objects made from recycled plastic items.

- Take a trip to your local landfill where plastic garbage is buried and have the staff explain the landfill process.

Discussion Questions:

- How exactly do toxins from a landfill get into soil and water? Trace the pollution process from a single buried plastic bottle of bleach to your water faucet.

- Invite a local recycling or waste management representative to come to your class and talk about their work; how much money does your local government allocate to recycling and sanitation services?

- How is plastic made? Research the chemical process that converts petroleum, gas and coal into plastic.

Stage Set:

a school lunch room with a plastic table and 2 plastic chairs

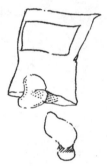

Cast:

8 actors, min. Saundra, Riley, Students 1–6

Effect:

sound—bell or buzzer ringing

Props:

book; sunglasses; juice bottle; potato chips; potato chip container; plastic food dish; soft-drink bottle; laundry detergent bottle; vegetable oil bottle; bread bag; yogurt cup; styrofoam food container; large plastic bag containing these items—drinking straw; toothbrush; pill bottle; lid; egg carton; garden hose section; fishing line; sewing thread spool; packing peanuts

Costumes:

characters wear contemporary school clothes with Saundra wearing a light jacket over her recycling code t-shirt; each Student 1–6 wears a t-shirt that has on the front a corresponding number inside the triangular plastic recycling code symbol—Student 1 has #1, Student 2 has #2, etc.; Saundra has #7 under her jacket.

(LIGHTS UP FULL ON SAUNDRA and RILEY sitting at a lunch table at down center. Saundra is reading a book; Riley is eating lunch.)

Saundra: Hi, Riley. I bet you a potato chip I can name more plastic things in this room than you can.

Riley: You don't have a potato chip, Saundra.

Saundra: I know—but you do, and I want one.

Riley: (offers a chip) Well, here—

Saundra: No! I want to earn it, not just have you give it to me!

Riley: You sound like my parents. You're scaring me!

Saundra: Come on, look around! Name whatever things you see made of plastic!

Riley: Ummm, your sunglasses—the lenses and the frame.

Saundra: This pen.

Riley: This table.

Saundra: These chairs.

Riley: This juice bottle.

Saundra: That potato chip container.

Riley: Ummm, I can't think of any more.

Saundra: No more? (points) How about that CD in Marsha's Walkman? (points) And the plastic knife and fork Derek is using to attack his spaghetti? (points) And the sack Deirdre's carrying her lunch in? (points) And the comb Benny's using to mess up his hair? And the gloves the food servers are wearing? And the covering over the ceiling lights? And Mr. Morton's hearing aid? And the trim on Darren's new sneakers? And Barbara's belt? And

Monika's earrings? And Janna's tennis racket? And the fill inside your jacket? All of it is plastic!

Riley: Okay, okay, you win. Here's your chip! You earned it!

Saundra: Thank you. (regards chip thoughtfully) What are you going to do with that plastic juice bottle when you're done with it?

Riley: Toss it! I mean, in an approved waste container. I wouldn't ever litter.

Saundra: Of course not. But do you know what happens to that bottle after you've put it in the trash?

Riley: No, but I bet you're going to tell me.

(Students 1–3 enter from right and stand at down right; Students 4–6 enter from left and stand at down left; each student carries a plastic object—Student 1, soft-drink bottle; Student 2, laundry detergent bottle; Student 3, vegetable oil bottle; Student 4, bread bag; Student 5, yogurt cup; Student 6, styrofoam food container.)

Student 1: Recycling is the process of collecting, sorting and then re-making a waste item to be used again.

Student 2: Either as a new product—

Student 3: Or back to its original form.

Student 4: Recycling helps preserve our environment and save natural resources.

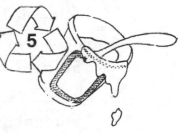

Riley: How?

Student 5: By using less land for dumping our garbage. Each year in the United States, nearly three million acres of farmland and more than one hundred seventy thousand acres of wetland disappear.

Student 6: Each day more than seven thousand acres of open space are lost forever.

Saundra: Less waste means less pollution. And less pollution means a better world.

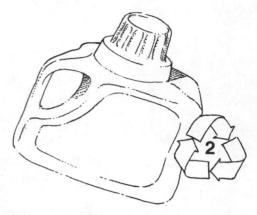

Riley: Well, what is plastic, anyway? Why doesn't it just go away when you throw it in the trash?

Student 1: The English word "plastic" comes from an ancient Greek word that means "to mold or to form."

Student 2: Modern plastic is a material that is very easy to mold or form into any shape, size and color.

Student 3: Plastic is made from a chemical compound called a polymer that is produced from oil.

Student 4: Plastic is light in weight but very strong and durable.

Student 5: And that's the problem with plastic—it just doesn't go away!

Student 6: Americans use two-point-five million plastic bottles every hour!

Student 1: Each person in the United States uses almost two hundred pounds of plastic a year!

Student 2: Most of our plastic trash gets buried in landfills.

Student 3: Some plastic is degradable, meaning it will decay after a few months or years.

Student 4: But most plastic never decays; when it's buried underground in a landfill, it can last forever!

Student 5: And if the plastic contains toxins—or poisons—it can escape into the land and water and kill our crops and animals.

Student 6: Recycling isn't just a good idea; it's a matter of life or death to the environment!

Saundra: The plastics industry has worked hard to solve this problem. They developed a system that tells what kind of plastic something is made of. And that makes it easier to recycle!

Riley: I see. Each type of plastic has its own number—like a code!

Saundra: And you find the numbers stamped on the bottom of the bottle or printed on the package.

(Students 1–6 display their plastic item and the place where the code number is found.)

Student 1: Code Number 1 is labeled PET. That's plastic made from a material called polyethylene terephthalate. It's used to make soft-drink and juice and water bottles.

Student 2: Code Number 2 is labeled HDPE. That's plastic made from high-density polyethylene. It's used to make milk jugs and laundry detergent bottles.

Student 3: Code Number 3 is labeled V. That's plastic made from vinyl and polyvinyl chloride. It's used to make vegetable oil bottles.

Student 4: Code Number 4 is labeled LDPE. That's plastic made from low-density polyethylene. It's used to make dry cleaning bags and bread bags.

Student 5: Code Number 5 is labeled PP. That's plastic made from polypropylene. It's used to make yogurt cups.

Student 6: Code Number 6 is labeled PS. That's plastic made from polystyrene. It's used to make styrofoam food containers.

Saundra: (opens her jacket and displays t-shirt with #7) And Code Number 7 is labeled "Other." That covers all the plastic made from all other materials (holds up a plastic food dish). This microwave food dish, for example.

Riley: That's all pretty cool. But what happens when this plastic juice bottle gets picked up from the recycling bin?

(Students 1–6 mime motions as they describe recycling process.)

Student 1: When it gets to a recycling plant and has been sorted with other plastic items in its category, the bottle gets chopped up by a high-speed grinding machine.

Student 2: Chopped up into little flakes and then cleaned off with a water spray machine.

Student 3: The flakes are put into a giant tumble dryer and dried out.

Student 4: These dried flakes may be melted down—

Student 5: Or molded into long sticky strands—

Student 6: Or shaped into tiny pellets.

Saundra: The recycled plastic is made into new products.

Riley: Such as?

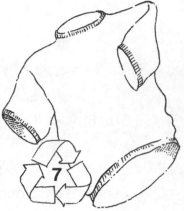

Student 1: Skis and surfboards.

Student 2: Flower pots and automobile parts.

Student 3: Pens and rulers.

Student 4: Park benches and picnic tables.

Student 5: Pipes and crates.

Student 6: Filling for sleeping bags and carpet.

Student 1: Pillows and jackets.

Student 2: Yard fencing and house insulation.

Student 3: Videotape cases.

Student 4: Shopping bags.

Student 5: Medicine capsules.

Student 6: Food trays.

Riley: And other new bottles.

Saundra: Now you get the idea!

Riley: Gosh, with recycling, we'd have all the plastic we need. We'd never have to make any new plastic at all!

Saundra: Unfortunately, only about one percent of all the plastic we use is recycled.

Riley: That's crazy!

Students 1–6: But it's true!

Riley: Well, what can we do to help people learn about recycling plastic?

Saundra: You can find out how to recycle in your own community. Call your town or city government and ask about their recycling program.

Student 1: And get your family and friends to recycle with you.

Student 2: When you buy a plastic item, make sure it's marked with a recycling code number.

Student 3: And try to buy things you're not going to just throw away after using them once.

(Saundra draws a large plastic bag from behind the table and pulls items from it, laying them on the table as they are announced by Students 1–6.)

Saundra: Best of all—because it's the most fun—you can be your own plastic recycler, right in your own home!

Student 4: Clean off your plastic drinking straws and use them to make mobiles and flower stems.

Student 5: Use your recycled toothbrush as a stencil brush.

Student 6: Use plastic lids as coasters.

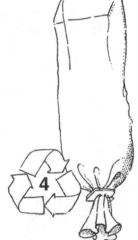

Student 1: Use egg cartons as extra ice cube trays or in the garden as seed starters for new plants.

Student 2: Cut up your old garden hose and use it as a pail handle.

Student 3: Or grips for your bicycle handlebars.

Student 4: Fishing line is great for hanging things from your ceiling.

Student 5: Sewing thread spools make great chess pieces.

Student 6: And those packing peanuts? They make great stuffing for toys.

Saundra: And don't forget about plastic milk bottles—they make great bird feeders!

(Sound: Bell or buzzer rings. Students 1–3 begin exiting right; Students 4–6 begin exiting left.)

Student 1: Oh, no, recess is over!

Student 4: See you after school!

Riley: Say, when we go back to class, why don't we see if our teacher will let us come up with ideas about how to make things out of recycled plastic?

Saundra: That's a good idea. Because if we don't learn how to recycle, when we grow up, we'll be buried by our garbage!

Riley: Lunch with you, Saundra, is always a learning experience.

(Saundra and Riley begin exiting left.)

Saundra: Did you know that Americans create 190 million tons of garbage a year! That weighs more than thirty million elephants! Each one of us produces an average of almost four pounds of garbage a day!

(They exit; LIGHTS OUT.)

THE END

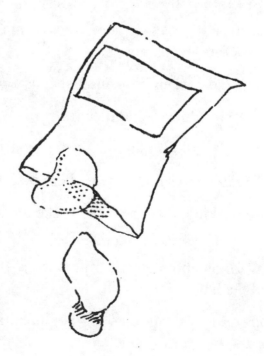

The Case of the Uncooked Eggs

by Myka-Lynn Sokoloff

CAST:
Bus Driver
Nicole
Monique
Odette
Jeanne
Soldier
Market Woman
Farmer
Messenger
Schoolteacher
Judge
Lawyer 1
Lawyer 2
Poor Man

SETTING:
A Small Town in Haiti

Bus Driver: Attention, s'il vous plaît! This is Petionville, the last stop this bus will make before returning to Port-au-Prince. Passengers on the roof, wait your turn. Make sure you have all your parcels and livestock before leaving the bus! *Merci!*

Nicole: Cousin Monique! Monique! Here I am, over here!

Monique: Nicole, it's so good to see you again!

Nicole: Cousins should see each other more than once every ten years! How was your trip out from Port-au-Prince?

Monique: Ah! This new bus service is wonderful. Remember how long the walk used to be? But so much has changed in the last ten years! I hardly recognized the village as we drove through it.

Odette: Do you recognize me, Monique?

Monique: Of course I do, Odette! How could I forget my cousin's best friend. So tell me, did some rich farmer move into town?

Odette: Rich farmer? What do you mean?

Monique: As we were coming into the village, we passed such a prosperous farm on the outskirts of town. I couldn't believe the sugarcane and bananas, the rows of yams, the large barn, and all the animals! Why, it looks like one of the finest farms in the region.

Nicole: Yes, everyone who sees the place makes the same comment. Do you remember how it looked the last time you were here?

Monique: I certainly do! What a ramshackle place it was—just a small thatched shack with a leaky roof and a crumbling, old barn. As I remember, it belonged to a poor widow whose name was Jeanne. How did this transformation take place?

© Macmillan/McGraw-Hill

Nicole: Ah, that's one of my favorite stories! Odette and I will tell it to you as we walk home. You see, it all started like this. . . .

SOUND EFFECT: [knocking on door]

Jeanne: Bonjour, soldier. How can I help you?

Soldier: Bonjour, madame. I'm on leave and on my way home to visit my family. I've been walking all day, but I still have many kilometers to go. I was wondering if I could spend the night in your barn?

Jeanne: Oui, but of course! It's an old barn that leaks when it rains; however, some shelter is better than none at all. But first, come in and have a bite of supper with me. It's only a simple meal—beans and rice—but I would be pleased to have you share it with me.

Soldier: Merci. That's very kind of you.

Nicole: Before leaving the next morning, the soldier stopped at Jeanne's house to thank her for her hospitality.

Soldier: I have no money to pay you for your kindness, but I hope you'll accept these three eggs I happen to have in my knapsack. Perhaps you'll cook them for your breakfast. Au revoir, madame, and thank you again.

Nicole: And with that, the soldier tipped his cap and went on his way.

Jeanne: Three eggs! Ah, they'd make a fine omelette, and, to tell the truth, I am a bit hungry. But, on the other hand, if I put them under a hen for a few days, perhaps they'll hatch. Yes, that's what I'll do.

Odette: Each day, Jeanne checked the eggs to see if anything had happened. On the third day, her hopes were realized.

Jeanne: Well, well! My three fine eggs have hatched into three fine chicks. When they are full grown, I'll sell them at the market for a good price.

Nicole: The chicks pecked in the dirt and scratched for grubs in the garden. Since Jeanne and I were old friends, I gave the chicks a little grain when I had some to spare, and in a few short months, they grew into sturdy roosters.

Odette: One day, we saw Jeanne heading for the marketplace. She was walking along the road with a basket on her head. Long tail feathers drooped over the sides of the basket.

Market Woman: Bananas for sale! Bananas and yams!

Jeanne: Your produce looks delicious, but I'm not interested in buying today. I want to sell my roosters.

Market Woman: In that case, go and talk to my husband over there; he may want to buy them.

Farmer: Jeanne, let me see the birds you're selling. I'm always in the market for roosters.

Jeanne: Then wait till you see the ones I've got in this basket—three of the finest roosters that ever crowed!

Farmer: Oui, these are indeed fine birds. Will you take a silver coin apiece for them?

Jeanne: No, my friend, one silver coin is not enough. These are no ordinary roosters—one look at their long tail feathers should tell you that! My birds are worth at least two coins apiece.

Farmer: You drive a hard bargain, Jeanne. Five silver coins for the three birds is all I can afford.

Jeanne: All right, I'll accept your price for the birds, with the understanding that I may keep the basket in which I carried them.

Farmer: What are you going to buy to put in your basket, Jeanne? Some bright fabric and ribbon?

Jeanne: No, indeed. I'm going to get two little piglets that I can raise into sleek, fat sows!

Monique: With five silver coins jingling in her pocket, it's hard to believe that Jeanne was able to resist the temptations of the market.

Nicole: Well, Monique, resist she did! Jeanne returned home with two wiggling, squealing piglets in her basket. Anyway, to make a long story short, she fed the piglets scraps from her table and garden, and before long they were fat enough to sell.

Odette: Do you remember how they got loose and rooted all through my garden? I had no yams to speak of that season! I certainly was happy the day I saw Jeanne herding those pigs to the marketplace.

Market Woman: Sisal rope and molasses for sale! Sisal rope. . . . Oh, Jeanne! It's good to see you back at the market. Come—take a look at my fine fabric! How long has it been since you've had a new skirt?

Jeanne: Your fabric is beautiful, and it's been a very long time since I've had anything new. But I must sell before I can buy.

Market Woman: Well, if you're interested in selling those pigs, go talk to my husband.

Farmer: Bonjour, Jeanne, what have you got to sell today?

Jeanne: I've got two fine, fat sows who will bear many young piglets. But I must warn you, I'm expecting to get a good price for them! These are no ordinary pigs.

Farmer: They certainly look healthy and plump. I'll tell you what I'll do; I'll make you an offer of ten silver coins for the two of them!

Jeanne: No, indeed. I know they're worth more than that. The least I'd accept is fifteen coins for the pair.

Farmer: Jeanne, you always strike such a hard bargain! Why don't we compromise? I'll give you twelve coins and ask my wife to give you some of her new sisal rope.

Jeanne: All right; that's a fair trade.

Monique: And did Jeanne use the money to buy herself a new skirt?

Nicole: No, indeed. Instead, she looked at every goat in the market and picked out the finest one that her twelve silver coins would purchase. That afternoon, we saw Jeanne leading her goat home on a long sisal rope. The goat gnawed on the rope as they walked along the road.

Odette: That goat would eat anything! It ate the sleeve of my favorite blouse that was hanging on the clothesline! See, here's the patch I had to sew.

Nicole: The goat did turn out to be a good milker, though. Our neighbor sold some of the milk and made cheese with the rest. In a few months, she was ready to barter the goat. So back to the market she went to talk to the farmer who had purchased her roosters and her sows.

Jeanne: We've traded together before. Now I'd like you to give me that calf in exchange for this goat and three crates of my delicious cheese.

Farmer: I'd call that an even trade!

Odette: Jeanne brought the calf home and fed it a bucketful of grain each day. In my opinion, it was the only well-behaved animal she ever owned. Anyway, over time the calf turned into a strong ox. Finally, the time came when it was ready to be taken back to the marketplace.

Farmer: Jeanne, what a handsome ox you have raised! It's young, but I believe it's sturdy enough to pull my plow. How much will you sell it for?

© Macmillan/McGraw-Hill

Jeanne: Give me a sackful of coins—enough to buy some land and some seed so I can plant my own corn and beans. If my harvests are good, perhaps someday I'll be able to buy another ox to plow my own fields.

Nicole: With the money, Jeanne bought some land and planted it. She worked hard, and her efforts were rewarded. She used the money she got from selling her crops to buy more animals and more land.

Monique: And did her good fortune change her?

Odette: Not in the least! In spite of her wealth, Jeanne lived very simply. When she could afford it, she painted her house and put a new tin roof on the barn. Through it all, she remained a good neighbor who was willing to help out anyone in need, even a stranger. And then one day, she heard a knock at the door.

SOUND EFFECT: [knocking on door]

Jeanne: Who is it?

Soldier: Bonjour, madame. I am a soldier on leave, passing through on my way home. Can you give me shelter for the night?

Jeanne: Oh-h-h, my goodness! Don't you recognize me? But then, why would you? It's been years since you passed this way before! The last time you stayed with me, I put you up in the barn. When you left the next morning, you gave me a gift of three eggs.

Soldier: Of course, now I remember you. But this can't be the place I stopped at before! Why, it was just a shack with a tumbledown barn; this is a prosperous farm. What has brought you such good fortune?

Jeanne: My dear sir, how happy I am that you've returned. There's so much to tell you—and so much to thank you for! Let me put on a pot of beans while I tell you my story.

The Case of the Uncooked Eggs 157

Nicole: What a stroke of luck that the soldier happened to return!

Odette: Well, I'm not so sure I would call it luck! Anyway, Jeanne prepared a fine meal for the soldier—oxtail soup, chicken, fried bananas, rice and beans, and coffee. When they sat down to eat, she told him what had happened to his gift of the three uncooked eggs.

Jeanne: . . . and so now you know how I managed to turn three eggs into all this! Please, you must stay with me and let me repay you for your generous gift by offering you my hospitality.

Monique: The soldier stayed with our Jeanne for five days, and she treated him royally. Each day, he wandered around her property, saying less and less and looking more and more thoughtful.

Nicole: That sounds like strange behavior for a guest! Did he give her another gift when he left?

Monique: No, he didn't. On the morning of the fifth day, the soldier went on his way after eating a hearty breakfast. According to Jeanne, the soldier thanked her, and said that he hoped he would see her again very soon. Then about a week later, there was another knock on Jeanne's door.

SOUND EFFECT: [knocking on door]

Jeanne: Oui? Who is it?

Messenger: I am a messenger of the court, madame. I have a summons for you.

Jeanne: A summons for me! In all my years, I've never received an official notice. You must have the wrong house. I'm sure this is for someone else.

Odette: Jeanne threw the paper away and let the entire matter slip from her mind. A week later, the same messenger reappeared.

SOUND EFFECT: [knocking on door]

Jeanne: Oh, I see you're back again. What have you brought me this time?

Messenger: It's another summons, madame.

Jeanne: How strange. Well, perhaps you'd better read it to me. What exactly does it say?

Messenger: "You are hereby summoned to appear in court to respond to a complaint brought against you."

Jeanne: Surely there is some mistake! There are many women in Haiti who have the name Jeanne. Perhaps you are confusing me with someone else. Please take your summons back to the court and explain to the judge that I'm a simple woman who has never done anything wrong.

Odette: One day, about a week later, Jeanne was working in her fields. I saw the messenger from the court come to her house and tack the summons up on the door. At this point, Jeanne knew she could ignore it no longer. She put on a clean dress and went to ask the village schoolteacher for his advice.

Jeanne: Schoolteacher, what should I do? I know I haven't committed any crimes. I'm not the woman they want!

Schoolteacher: Well, Madame Jeanne, this may be a case of mistaken identity, but I don't think you should ignore this summons. It says, "Failure to respond to this summons may result in imprisonment."

Jeanne: Oh, dear! What shall I do? That sounds serious.

Schoolteacher: It is serious. My nephew once got a summons to appear in court, and when he didn't show up, they came and took him away!

Jeanne: Oui, I've heard of such dreadful things happening.

Schoolteacher: My advice to you is to go to the courthouse in Port-au-Prince. You must settle this matter before someone comes to arrest you!

Nicole: So, what did Jeanne do?

Odette: What anyone in her place would do. She woke before the rooster crowed, put on her good dress, and tied a new scarf around her head. Then, carrying her shoes on her head so they wouldn't get dusty on the long walk, she set off to Port-au-Prince. When she arrived at the courthouse, the first person she saw was the soldier!

Nicole: The soldier? But what was he doing there? I thought he was going home on leave?

Monique: Ah, just wait until you hear! The clerk directed Jeanne to take a seat on a bench across from the soldier. Then the judge called for order in the court.

SOUND EFFECT: [gavel banging]

Judge: The court will now hear The Case of the Uncooked Eggs. Will the party who is bringing suit please step forward and identify himself?

Soldier: I am bringing this suit, Judge.

Judge: Against whom is your suit directed?

Soldier: Against that woman who is sitting on the bench across from me.

Judge: State the nature of your complaint.

Soldier: Several years ago, I gave this woman a gift, and, because of my generosity, she is a wealthy woman today. I am here to get what I feel is rightfully mine—a share of her riches.

Monique: What nerve! I can't believe the soldier actually said that!

Nicole: Neither could Jeanne!

Judge: We will now hear from the accused. Please come forward.

Jeanne: Your honored Judge, I cannot understand why this soldier is suing me, for I've taken nothing that is his. In fact, I gave him food and shelter!

Judge: Is this true, soldier?

Soldier: I once asked this woman for a night's shelter. She gave me a bite to eat and allowed me to sleep in her barn. To show my thanks, I gave her a gift of three eggs.

Judge: And why does that now entitle you to share this woman's wealth?

Soldier: When I met this woman, she had barely enough beans for an evening meal. Today she has flocks of chickens and a pasture filled with goats and cows. She has fields of corn, beans, and carrots, not to mention a garden of beautiful roses! She's a rich woman—all because of the eggs I gave her. It is only fair that she share her wealth with me!

Judge: Madame, how do you respond to this?

Jeanne: Well, Your Honor, the soldier did not give me my animals, my land, or my money. He gave me only three eggs! Everything that I have today, I earned through my own hard work.

Monique: Oui, Jeanne spoke the truth—what's right is right! Surely you'll tell me that the judge dismissed the case?

Odette: Alas for our poor friend Jeanne, he did not.

Judge: This is indeed a complicated case that will have to be properly tried. I, therefore, order you both to have lawyers prepare arguments to present in court. This case is adjourned for two weeks.

Nicole: And so, Jeanne hired a lawyer to defend her. Two weeks later, she and the soldier both reappeared in court with their lawyers.

Odette: But this time, according to what Jeanne told us, the soldier's story sounded very different.

SOUND EFFECT: [gavel banging]

Judge: This court is now in session. The court will hear The Case of the Uncooked Eggs. The lawyer for the soldier may speak first.

Lawyer 1: Merci, Your Honor. I call my client to the witness stand to tell us how he first met this woman.

Soldier: Well, sir, a few years ago, I asked this woman for a night's shelter. She fed me a few burned beans for dinner and gave me a bed of wet straw under her leaky barn roof. However, having a generous nature, I rewarded her with a bountiful gift of three large eggs.

Lawyer 1: And did this stingy woman appreciate your gift?

Lawyer 2: Your Honor, I object! There is nothing to indicate that my client is stingy! In fact, my evidence will show that her generosity is well known.

Judge: Objection sustained. Proceed.

Lawyer 1: Well, then, what happened when you saw this woman again?

Soldier: I learned that it was my gift that had led to her wealth! Imagine my surprise! It was clear that I deserved more than just her gratitude.

Lawyer 1: And what do you feel would be fair payment for starting this woman on the road to riches?

Soldier: I only seek what is just—nothing more. I would accept half her land and livestock, for without my gift she would still be poor.

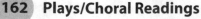

© Macmillan/McGraw-Hill

Judge: You may step down. The court will now hear from the lawyer for the accused.

Lawyer 2: Your Honor, though my client was very poor, she treated the soldier with generosity. In return, he gave her a gift—a gift that she could use in any way she saw fit. It was her hard work, not the eggs, that brought her wealth. I now call my client to speak on her own behalf.

Odette: And so, it was Jeanne's turn to tell her story.

Monique: Finally! And then the judge ruled in her favor, oui?

Nicole: No! The case went on and on as the two lawyers argued. At last, on Friday afternoon, the judge said he would announce his decision the following Monday.

Odette: That evening, after Jeanne had returned home, I stopped by her house to see how she was feeling.

Jeanne: Oh, my friend, I am exhausted! If someone were to drop a handkerchief on me, I would fall to the floor! I am almost willing to divide my property with the soldier rather than face that courtroom another day.

Odette: I begged her not to lose heart; after all, the trial was almost over. As we spoke, a stranger appeared at the door.

Poor Man: Excuse me, madame. Will you offer charity to a poor man? Can you spare a little something for me to eat?

Jeanne: Please go away! I'm not giving out charity today, for tomorrow I may have nothing!

Poor Man: I'm sorry to hear that. What's troubling you so, if I may ask?

Odette: Well, Jeanne told the poor man her story. By the time she finished, she had relented about turning him away. You see, it was not in her nature to be unkind.

Jeanne: Ah, well, my troubles aren't your fault. Come in and let me find some rice and beans for your supper.

Poor Man: Merci, madame. Perhaps I can repay your kindness with some advice. Eat well on Saturday and Sunday. Get up early Monday morning, make yourself coffee, and walk to the city. I will be waiting for you in the courtroom.

Jeanne: You will be waiting for me? But what can you do?

Poor Man: You shall see.

Monique: Did Jeanne follow the man's advice?

Odette: Oui, she did. She was up very early Monday morning, long before the rooster crowed. She made coffee and then started out on the long walk to Port-au-Prince. Since it was such an important day, Nicole and I accompanied her to court. When we arrived, the poor man was already seated on one of the benches in the rear.

SOUND EFFECT: [gavel banging]

Judge: Today I will hear the final arguments in the Case of The Uncooked Eggs. The soldier's lawyer will begin.

Lawyer 1: Merci, Your Honor. Allow me to call attention once again to the most praiseworthy character of my client, and to his . . .

Odette: The lawyer droned on and on and on. Half the people in the courtroom, including the judge, were dozing in the heat. The other half were watching the flies buzz around the ceiling fan.

Nicole: When at last the soldier's lawyer concluded, Jeanne's lawyer spoke—and spoke and spoke. Finally, he finished. Then came the moment we had all been waiting for!

Judge: I have heard the evidence presented by both sides, and I have reached a verdict.

Odette: From his bench in the back of the courtroom, the poor man stood up, calling out and waving his cane.

Poor Man: Judge! One moment, please!

Judge: What is it, old man?

Poor Man: May I move up to the front, the better to hear the verdict?

Judge: Why should a poor man, such as yourself, be interested in my verdict for this case?

Poor Man: Allow me to explain, Your Honor. A few days ago, this good woman gave me a dinner of rice and beans as an act of charity.

Judge: So? What significance could your dinner possibly have for this court?

Poor Man: I will tell you: I ate the rice, but took the beans home to plant. When I told a friend, he offered me space in his field. He is, at this very moment, in the field waiting for me. And I am here waiting for your decision. I want to know whether it is worth the trouble for me to plant my beans.

Judge: Old man, whoever heard of planting cooked beans?

Poor Man: Well, Judge, this good woman told me this court believed that eggs could produce flowers and pigs and goats. So I thought perhaps I, too, should make the effort. After all, if the laws have been changed and eggs can give all that, just think what beans can do!

Judge: Hmmm. . . . Your statement has made this case quite clear to me. The court rules that the soldier's claim is unfounded, unwarranted, and unreasonable. Case dismissed!

Monique: So Jeanne won! Bravo!

Odette: Oui! The next day, Jeanne gave a big party to celebrate. And the guest of honor was none other than the poor man whose cleverness had won the case for her.

Nicole: All the neighbors came, and what a feast there was—goat stew, chicken and chili, saffron rice, fruit, and cakes galore. But there was one thing missing from the menu, and can you guess what it was?

All: EGGS!

A Visit from an Ancient Pharaoh

by Carolyn Clark

CAST:

The Archaeologist

Archaeology Assistants:
Andrea, John, Karen, Roberto

Hatshepsut

Senemut (SEN uh mut)

Royal Guard (up to 4 students)

© Macmillan/McGraw-Hill

Hatshepsut (hat SHEP soot) was the best known and most powerful female pharaoh of Egypt. She came to the throne in 1503 B.C. when her husband, Thutmose II, died. Her stepson, Thutmose III, was too young to accept the responsibilities of being pharaoh, so Hatshepsut and Thutmose III ruled together in name. However, the power of the throne belonged to Hatshepsut. Before Hatshepsut became ruler, Egypt often conquered other nations in order to gain wealth and power. How was Hatshepsut's reign different?

Play begins with The Archaeologist in the front as if lecturing before an audience, assistants in background, sitting still in "digging" positions. Hatshepsut and other ancient Egyptian characters are offstage.

The Archaeologist: Good afternoon, ladies and gentlemen. Thank you for asking me here today to share my recent archaeological findings from ancient Egypt. As you will see, my team and I found much more than we expected. Our adventure began as we were digging for artifacts from around 1500 B.C. . . . [The Archaeologist joins assistants.]

Andrea: How long have we been here?

The Archaeologist: Three months, two weeks, and one day.

John: Seems like since the time of the pharaohs!

Karen: And all we've found is . . .

All Assistants Together: SAND!!

Roberto: Sand in my shoes!

Andrea: Sand in my hair!

John: Sand in my sandwich!

Karen: Sand in my . . .

The Archaeologist: [interrupting and pointing at a pottery jar] Wait! I think I've found something here!

Andrea: It's about time!

Roberto: What is it?

The Archaeologist: It looks like pottery. A jar, maybe, but let's leave it right where it is, for now.

John: I'll get the camera so that we can take a photograph of the object in the spot where we found it.

Karen: Here's the whisk brush. I'll help you clean it.

Andrea: I can check the exact ground level. [Karen brushes off the jar. John photographs the jar. Andrea studies a chart on a clipboard.]

The Archaeologist: This looks like it could be from the Pharaoh Hatshepsut's era, but we'll have to use carbon-14 dating on it when we get back to the lab to be sure. That will tell us the level of radioactive carbon within the pottery and help us determine its age.

Roberto: [carefully picking up the jar] Look! It is a jar.

Karen: [sniffing] Aah, I smell something really sweet.

Andrea: Yes, like perfume, or incense.

John: It's coming from inside the jar. It smells wonderful!

The Archaeologist: What you are smelling is myrrh, which comes from the sticky resin of a tree. It was used as incense in ancient times.

John: Well, whatever it is, I feel like something important is about

to happen. [Hatshepsut enters and very slowly crosses the stage holding onto Senemut's arm. They are surrounded by a royal guard.]

Karen: Me, too. Am I dreaming, or is there some lady dressed in gold coming toward us right now?

Roberto: If you're dreaming, then so am I, and it's a strange dream. She looks like an ancient Egyptian!

Andrea: And look at all those people around her. They look pretty ancient, too.

John: Maybe it's a costume party.

Andrea: In the middle of the desert?

Karen: Look around, Andrea. This is really weird, but we're not in the desert anymore. We're on the banks of a river, and I think it's the Nile.

The Archaeologist: [slowly, through clenched teeth] I am a scientist. These things don't happen to scientists.

Roberto: Calm down, Professor. Here they come.

Royal Guard Member I: Can we arrest them, please, your Majesty?

Royal Guard Member II: Oh, come on, we haven't arrested anybody in almost 3,500 years.

Royal Guard Member III: They look dangerous to me!

Hatshepsut: [smiles at archaeology crew, then turns back to the soldiers] Royal Guard! We will not arrest these people unless they threaten us. I know you are frustrated because I have never sent you into battle, but I will not allow any violence from you, except in self-defense! Besides, these are people of good will. I've been watching them for months.

John: You've been watching us? Excuse me, but who are you?

Hatshepsut: I am Hatshepsut, pharaoh of Egypt. This [indicates the person beside her] is Senemut, my trusted advisor, and these are members of my royal guard.

The Archaeologist: Your majesty, I would like to know how you managed to appear here today. I would also like to know why we started out our day in the desert and ended up standing on the banks of the Nile River. But I won't ask because I am a scientist, and as a scientist, I am sure I must be imagining the whole thing.

Hatshepsut: [smiles mysteriously and shrugs] As you wish.

Andrea: Well, I think she's real, and I have a question. You're a woman. How did you become pharaoh of Egypt?

Hatshepsut: Is that really so strange to you? My father was pharaoh. My husband was pharaoh. I am of royal blood and trained to be a leader. My culture has goddesses, why not a female pharaoh?

Karen: Then why are you the only woman pharaoh I've ever heard of?

Hatshepsut: It is true that men were favored as leaders. But when my husband died,

the only other choice for pharaoh was my stepson, Thutmose. He was only a child—certainly not ready to be ruler of Egypt. I agreed to let him share the title of pharaoh with me. But the power was mine.

Karen: Didn't the men object?

Hatshepsut: No ruler is popular with everyone. I did what I could to prove that a good leader is a good leader, male or female. That's why, when you see statues of me, sometimes I am shown as a woman and sometimes as a sphinx, with my head on the body of a lion. At other times I am shown as a man—with a big, heavy beard! [Hatshepsut strokes her chin and shakes her head.]

John: Please tell us why you are here.

Hatshepsut: When I first noticed you digging in the sand, I didn't know what you were doing. I thought you might be treasure hunters or grave robbers. Then when you found my jar of myrrh, I saw how carefully you treated it. The jar isn't valuable, so I realized you were looking for knowledge, not gold. And I knew you could see my beloved Egypt much more clearly with my help.

Roberto: [pointing into the distance] Look! Over there at the river! Ships! [Everyone looks toward imaginary river.]

Hatshepsut: Yes, those are my ships. Five beautifully crafted, wooden sailing ships returning from the land of Punt. They were gone for two years. Instead of sending out military expeditions, I sent out trade expeditions. We took goods that we had in surplus—like papyrus, jewelry, and bronze weapons—and exchanged them for things we had too little of. We traded a certain amount of our goods for an equal value of their goods. That way we all got what we needed, as well as things for pleasure, too!

John: Can we see what they brought?

Hatshepsut: Of course! [speaking to one of the royal guard members] Royal guard member! Go and get some of the jewels from Punt!

Royal Guard Member: Yes, your majesty. [Royal guard member exits.]

Andrea: Why are all those soldiers getting off the ships? I thought you said this wasn't a military expedition.

Hatshepsut: My soldiers helped with the trade expeditions. They enjoyed it, and it kept them occupied in peaceful activities.

Karen: Look! There's an artist, drawing a picture of the whole scene. Who are those other people—the ones who are writing?

Hatshepsut: Those are scribes. Some wrote down the events of the day, while others

A Visit from an Ancient Pharaoh 173

kept account of the goods that came from the ships.

Roberto: They're starting to unload the cargo. I see boxes of gold, and elephant tusks.

John: And leopard skins, and is that . . . [pointing] . . . is that a family of chimpanzees?

The Archaeologist: Those look like very important people getting off the ship right now, but they aren't dressed like Egyptians. Who are they?

Hatshepsut: They are important representatives from the land of Punt. I'm glad they returned with the expedition. Their customs were different from ours, but we respected each other's differences. I enjoyed meeting with them.

Karen: There's that marvelous perfume smell again. Mmmmmmm.

Hatshepsut: Myrrh and frankincense. Those are the best fragrances in the world. Oh, they are unloading my myrrh trees! I asked for eighty-one myrrh trees to plant around my temple at Deir al-Bahri [DER el BAHR ee].

Senemut: I designed the temple. I wanted her majesty to have a beautiful monument to be remembered by. Unfortunately, young Thutmose destroyed much of the evidence of her majesty's existence. I was never able to finish the temple.

Hatshepsut: Yes, Thutmose. I hate to say too much—he was my stepson. But Thutmose certainly did long for power, and he sometimes used it in destructive ways. However, the most important monument to me is not made from stone. It is a message made from the lessons of history and passed on through each generation.

Andrea: [softly] What is the message, your majesty?

Hatshepsut: The message I wish to hear echoing through history is this: The wealth of my empire did not depend on conquering other nations. It depended on cooperation with other nations. We traded the things we had plenty of and got what we needed in return. Our lives were made richer. Other nations were made richer, and we could live alongside each other in peace. Leaving this knowledge to the world will stand as my monument. Will you help me? Will you be my messengers?

Archaeologist and Assistants: Yes, your majesty. [Royal guard member returns carrying jewels.]

Hatshepsut: Thank you. [taking jewels from the royal guard member and handing them to The Archaeologist] Please take these jewels as a token of my appreciation. We believe they will bring you luck.

The Archaeologist:	Pharaoh, we are grateful to you. We will try to make your voice from the past become a voice of the future.
Hatshepsut and Senemut:	Goodbye!
Archaeologist and Crew:	Goodbye! [Everyone but The Archaeologist exits—ancient Egyptians to one side, archaeology crew to the other. The Archaeologist comes back to center and faces audience.]
The Archaeologist:	Did we really see Hatshepsut? My scientific training tells me it is impossible, and no scientific journal would ever accept my story. But we have her jewels, and more importantly, we have her message: Nations can live together in peace.

THE END

After Hatshepsut's death in 1483 B.C., Thutmose III became the sole pharaoh. He attempted to remove all traces of Hatshepsut's life and influence. Unlike Hatshepsut, whose reign was mostly peaceful, Thutmose III became known as one of the world's first great generals. He returned to the idea of gaining wealth and power through force. He led many military campaigns and extended Egypt's rule to the Euphrates River. Thutmose died in 1450 B.C.

Tennessee Tornado

by Susan Strane

CAST:
Wilma Present
Mama
Wilma Past
Doctor
Mrs. Hoskins
Yvonne
Teammate 2
Teammate 3
Teammate 4
Woman
Man
Coach Gray
Teammate 1
Coach Temple
Mae Faggs
Judge
Young Boy

Wilma Present: I was nicknamed the "Tennessee Tornado" by the press, but my friends and family back in my hometown of Clarksville, Tennessee, knew me as just plain Wilma Rudolph. There were twenty-two kids in my family, and I was number twenty. My daddy, Ed Rudolph, worked as a railroad porter. In his spare time, he did odd jobs for people around town. My mama, whose name was Blanche, cleaned houses to make extra money. Both of them worked hard to support our large family; still, when I think back on it, we had very little money. There were lots of things we did without, but one thing we did have plenty of was love. Born on June 23, 1940, I was a premature baby, tipping the scales at just four and a half pounds. Maybe that was why I was always sick when I was growing up.

Mama: Wilma, honey, sometimes I think you've had more than your fair share of being sick. Why, you're only three years old, and you've already had the measles, the chicken pox, the mumps, and I don't know how many colds!

Wilma Past: Does that mean I'm special, Mama?

Mama: Maybe it does, child. Here, now drink this down.

Wilma Past: Oh, Mama, do I have to? I hate that stuff!

Mama: Do you want to get well?

Wilma Past: Yes!

Mama: Then drink it and get under those covers. Go on now; swallow every last drop!

Wilma Present: In spite of my mother's concoctions, I never had the strength that other kids had. Every cold I got seemed to last for weeks, and then it would develop into something else. When I was four, I had double pneumonia complicated by scarlet fever. That was one time Mama put her home remedies aside and called the doctor.

Mama: She'll be all right, won't she, Doctor?

Doctor: She'll recover from the pneumonia and the scarlet fever, Mrs. Rudolph. But I'm afraid she contracted polio while she was ill. As a result, one of her legs is partially paralyzed. I'm sorry to have to tell you this, but I doubt that she'll ever walk again.

Wilma Past: I will walk again. I will! I will!

Mama: Yes, you will, child. We're going to fight this thing, you understand? Don't you worry, everything is going to turn out all right.

Wilma Present: I started wearing a heavy metal brace to keep my leg straight. The brace went on as soon as I got up, and I wasn't allowed to take it off until I went to bed. When I was six, my mother and I started going to a hospital in Nashville for physical therapy. Twice each week, month after month, year after year—for four long years—I went for treatments. It was fifty miles each way in the back of a bus, which was the only place black people were allowed to sit. Back then, in the 1940s, there was still segregation in the South.

Mama: There's only one seat left. You sit down, Wilma.

Wilma Past: There are seats up front, Mama. It's not fair that you have to stand.

Mama: No, it's not fair, and it's not right. Maybe someday things will be different. But until that time, you just hold up your head and don't let anybody get you down.

Wilma Present: The treatments to strengthen my leg were painful. But even so, I looked forward to those trips to Nashville. I was getting out of Clarksville, seeing new things.

Wilma Past: I like traveling, Mama. Someday, I'm going to break out of this brace, and I'm going to see lots of new places.

Wilma Present: I guess I had big dreams even then. Sometimes after one of these trips, I would inspect my leg to see if I could detect any change. For a long time, I didn't notice any improvement.

Wilma Past: You've just got to be better by now, leg. That doctor works on you twice every week, and Mama massages you every night. There's got to be more to life than this. You hear me? Enough is enough!

Wilma Present: Yes, I started to get angry. I began to fight back in a new way. It was almost like a competition— me against my illness—and I was determined to win, no matter what!

Wilma Past: Mama, I'm seven years old now, and I can walk pretty well with my brace. You know how you and Daddy always say education is the most important thing? Well, I'm tired of being taught at home. I want to go to school with the other kids.

Mama: Wilma, honey, I know you've been dreaming about it for a long time. And goodness knows you've got a strong will.

Wilma Past: Same as you do, Mama!

Mama: Well, we'll try it out.

Wilma Present: I started school as a second grader. Despite all my brave talk, I must admit I felt terrified the first day I set foot in that school. Fortunately, my teacher was a warm, supportive person who sensed that I desperately needed to belong. She was in charge of the Brownies, and she urged me to join. That turned my life around. Fourth grade was another important year for me. I had a teacher named

Mrs. Hoskins. My, she was strict! But she taught me how to think positively, and I grew to love her.

Mrs. Hoskins: Wilma! How are you going to learn anything if you don't pay attention? Save your dreaming for when you sleep!

Wilma Past: Sorry, Mrs. Hoskins, I was just looking at Nancy's picture. I sure wish I could draw as pretty as that.

Mrs. Hoskins: Wilma, if you want to do something, do it. Don't daydream about it. Do it!

Wilma Present: By the time I was ten, everyone in town was used to seeing me with that brace. To them, it was a part of me. But not to me. One Sunday, we all went to church, like always. But it was a day I'll never forget.

Mama: Hurry along, now. Looks like everyone is already here, except us.

Wilma Past: You all go ahead in. I'll be along in a minute.

Yvonne: Come on, Mama. The service is about to begin.

Wilma Present: I waited a few minutes before I finally went in. I knew right away that people were staring at me. I could hear them buzzing as I walked down the aisle to where my family was sitting.

Woman: I do declare!

Man: I can't believe what my eyes are seeing!

Woman: Just look at that!

Yvonne: Mama! Daddy! It's Wilma!

Mama: Praise be! Wilma's walking down the aisle on her own two legs. Oh, happy, happy day!

Wilma Present: I had walked in without the brace. After church, a lot of people came over to congratulate me.

Man: That's tremendous, Wilma! You sure gave us a surprise!

Yvonne: You said you'd walk again, and you did it!

Wilma Present: I just smiled and beamed and didn't say much. But looking back on it, I'd say it was one of the most important moments of my life. Over the next two years, I wore the brace off and on as I regained the full use of my leg. Then, when I was in the sixth grade, Mama packed up the brace and sent it back to the hospital. Now that I had achieved my first goal, I set a new one for myself. I was determined to become someone special. That fall, I entered seventh grade, which turned out to be another pivotal year in my life.

Yvonne: Wilma, it's hard for me to believe that you'll be going to Burt High School with me this fall!

Wilma Present: For the kids I knew, everything revolved around Burt High School, where Clarksville's black students attended seventh through twelfth grades. Athletics were very important in the school, and most kids went out for a sport. My sister Yvonne was on the girls' basketball team, and I made up my mind to follow in her footsteps.

Wilma Past: Yvonne, do you think Coach Gray will give me a chance to play on the basketball team?

Yvonne: Wilma, what are you talking about? You don't know the first thing about basketball!

Wilma Past: That's what you think! I've been watching all of you play for years. I've studied every move. I know which ones work and which ones don't. And I'm getting real tall. What do you say, Mama?

Mama: Child, I'm not sure if you should go out for sports. What if you fall and get hurt? I can't bear to think of all those years of massage and therapy wasted.

© Macmillan/McGraw-Hill

Wilma Past: I'll be okay, Mama. I know I can do it!

Mama: Well, I guess there's no use trying to change your mind. Once you get set on something, there's no stopping you.

Wilma Present: I made the team, but thinking back on it, I'm fairly sure that Coach Clinton Gray selected me because of my sister. I didn't play one single minute of a game that entire season—I was a real "bench-warmer," you might say. However, I wasn't wasting time. I watched and studied everything that happened on the court. I practiced every spare minute.

Mama: Where you going, Wilma? It's almost dinner time.

Wilma Past: I'm just going out in the yard, Mama. I want to shoot some baskets. When Coach Gray puts me in a game, I've got to be ready, don't I?

Mama: I never did see anyone work so hard at a thing as you do, child.

Wilma Present: My mother was right. I practiced until I was shooting and rebounding better than most of my teammates. But even after three straight years, I never really got to show what I could do. Oh, I did get into some games, but only when there were a few seconds left, and the team was either way ahead or behind. I didn't complain, but sitting on the bench was getting harder and harder! At the end of my ninth-grade season, Coach Gray proposed a new idea to the team, but to our surprise, it had nothing to do with basketball.

Coach Gray: Listen up, girls! I'm thinking of starting a girls' track team. It'll help you stay in shape for basketball. Would any of you like to go out for it?

Wilma Past: Sure, Coach!

Teammate 1: Sounds good to me!

Coach Gray: Okay, we start on Monday.

Wilma Present: I figured track would give me something to do after school between basketball seasons. As it turned out, running was pure enjoyment for me. I had no knowledge about the technical aspects of the sport or even about the work involved. But I was fast, and I won about twenty races that spring without any effort on my part. At that point, my sister gave me some friendly advice.

Yvonne: Gee, Wilma, maybe you ought to spend more time on running than on basketball. You ought to go with your strongest sport.

Wilma Past: I love running, Yvonne, but it's just something to do in the spring. Basketball is still my favorite sport.

Wilma Present: When basketball season started in my sophomore year, I felt my time had come.

Wilma Past: Coach, I've been warming the bench for three seasons. I know I'm ready for a spot in the starting lineup. How about it?

Coach Gray: Wilma, you're more annoying than a "skeeter" buzzing 'round my head, but you've worked real hard. All right, I'll give you a try.

Wilma Past: Thanks, Coach. You won't be sorry!

Wilma Present: Coach Gray made me a starting player—finally! The nickname that he gave me, "Skeeter," slang for mosquito, also stuck. I'll never forget my very best game that season. I scored thirty-two points and didn't miss a single shot or free throw.

Coach Gray: You keep that up, Skeeter, and we'll make the championships this year.

Wilma Present: Coach Gray's prediction was right. Our team did make it into the Tennessee High School Girls' Championships. We won a tough game in our first round, but then our smugness got the better of us. We were defeated by eight points in a game marked by sloppy ball handling and poor defense. After the game, I was crushed. Little did I know that it would turn out to be one of the most significant experiences of my entire life.

Coach Temple: Excuse me, Wilma. I'd like to talk to you for a minute or two. My name's Ed Temple. I'm the coach for the Tigerbelles, the women's track team at Tennessee State University in Nashville.

Wilma Past: Yes, sir. Say, weren't you one of the referees tonight?

Coach Temple: Yes, I was. I do a lot of officiating so I can scout out new talent for my Tigerbelles. Based on what I saw tonight, I'd say you're definitely a new talent.

Wilma Past: Thank you, Mr. Temple, but I don't know how anyone could think that after the way I played tonight!

Coach Temple: Actually, Wilma, I'm thinking of another sport. With your height and long legs, you've got the makings of a sprinter. Have you ever considered competitive track?

Wilma Past: Not really, sir. I do a lot of running after basketball season is over, but we don't have a real track team at Burt High. We don't even have a track. We jog outside and, when it rains, we run through the school.

Coach Temple: Well, I know I can make a runner out of you. Just keep in mind what I've said, and we'll talk again sometime.

Wilma Present: So there I was in 1956—a fifteen-year-old high school sophomore with a life that revolved around basketball, running, and my family. I'd never been so happy. As soon as basketball season ended, I put on my track shoes and started running. I ran every minute I could. I'd gotten the taste of winning and found I liked it.

Coach Gray: Well, girls, next week is the big track meet at Tuskegee, Alabama.

Wilma Past: Who's gonna be there, Coach?

Coach Gray: You'll be competing against girls from all over the South. Only the best runners are invited.

Teammate 1: Wow! That must mean we're pretty good.

Coach Gray: You are, but I'd be kidding you if I didn't tell you that the competition is going to be tough, especially the girls from Atlanta, Georgia. They can practice all year round because of the warm climate there.

Wilma Past: Don't worry, Coach. We'll make you proud of us!

Wilma Present: When we got to the track, I saw that Coach Gray was right. The girls from Georgia really looked like runners. But I didn't pay much attention to them because, after my string of wins around Clarksville, I was feeling pretty cocky.

Wilma Past: I think I can beat them. After all, I've won every single race I've ever been in.

Teammate 1: I'll see you after the meet, Wilma. We're planning a big victory celebration.

Wilma Present: So what happened? I didn't win a single race! I was totally devastated. My speed was no match for the training and experience of the other girls entered in the meet. I went home and moped around. Then somewhere along the line, I realized that I had learned a very important lesson: Nobody goes through life undefeated. If you can pick up after a crushing defeat and go on to win again, you're going to be a champion someday. But if losing destroys you, it's all over.

Wilma Past: I've got to try to put it all back together. There's a lot more to track than running fast. I've got to learn the right way to run.

Wilma Present: I acquired this sense of determination that I would never, ever give up no matter what else happened. I won the rest of the races I was entered in that season, but I never forgot Tuskegee. In fact, I remember thinking that anybody who had seen me lose so badly at that meet would have written me off. To my surprise, I was wrong.

Coach Gray: Wilma, remember Ed Temple, the referee who's the women's track coach at Tennessee State? He's planning to come to Clarksville to talk with your folks.

Wilma Past: He is? What about?

Coach Gray: I think he wants you to spend the summer at the university, learning some running techniques.

Wilma Present: I rushed home to tell my mama and daddy.

Mama: Wilma, honey, you're too young to be leaving home.

Wilma Past: Mama, don't you see what a big break this is? If Coach Temple thinks I'm good enough, he might offer me a scholarship to the university. I could go to college!

Wilma Present: While my parents talked it over with Coach Temple, I just sat tight and held my breath.

Mama: Well, Wilma, you're the first one in this family who's ever had the chance to go to college. If running is going to do that, we just want you to put your mind to being the best you can be!

Wilma Present: That summer of 1956 was no vacation for me. I learned that raw speed was not enough to win races. Coach Temple taught me breathing techniques, race strategies, and how to blast out of the starting blocks. It was hard work all right, but the hardest lesson of all was learning mental toughness.

Coach Temple: Wilma, you're holding back when you run. I can see it.

Wilma Past: Gee, Coach, I'm just a high school kid. Those girls on the senior team are older. Some of them are real track stars. I feel it would be disrespectful, almost, if I beat them.

Coach Temple: Listen, Wilma, a track meet is not a popularity contest. Remember that! You're out there to win. So push for it!

Wilma Past: I'll try, Coach.

Coach Temple: You've got to do more than try, Wilma. You've got to change your mental attitude. I want you ready for the Amateur Athletic Union meet in Philadelphia, and that's only a few weeks away.

Wilma Past: Coach, I'll be ready! I wouldn't miss it for anything. I've always dreamed of traveling.

Wilma Present: We drove up to Philadelphia in a caravan of station wagons. I'd never been up North before. Everything in Philadelphia seemed so foreign to me. When we went to Franklin Stadium, I nearly fainted I was so intimidated.

Wilma Past: I've never seen a stadium this big! I feel like a midget.

Coach Temple: At six feet, you're some midget, Wilma!

Wilma Present: The weeks of intensive training paid off. I won nine races, and our relay team captured the junior title.

Coach Temple: You're coming along real well, Wilma. You've got a lot of potential.

Wilma Present: Right after the AAU meet in Philadelphia, Coach Temple and I had a long talk.

Coach Temple: You have a good possibility of making the women's Olympic track team this fall, Wilma. I think you should give it a try.

Wilma Past: That's a pretty big track meet, isn't it, Coach?

Coach Temple: It's more than a track meet. The Olympics are the oldest competitive games in the world. They were first held in Greece around 3,000 years ago. Every four years, the best amateur athletes from all over the world are chosen to compete.

Wilma Past: Did you say that athletes come from all over the world?

Coach Temple: That's right. This year the games will be held in Melbourne, Australia. You're just sixteen, but you might make it . . . if you push hard enough.

Wilma Past: After Philadelphia, I feel I can do anything!

Wilma Present: We started the first leg of our journey to Melbourne a couple of weeks later. Coach Temple drove me and a group of Tigerbelles to the Olympic tryouts in Seattle, Washington. One of these college stars was a woman named Mae Faggs. Mae held all sorts of records in women's track, and she had won medals in previous Olympics. She took a special interest in me from the first day we met.

Mae: Wilma, I'm going to give you some tough advice. Stop trying to fit in with everybody else. Stop worrying if someone is going to like you or not if you win. Start running like an individual.

Wilma Past: I'm just a high school kid. I don't want to cause any hard feelings.

Wilma Present: But Mae wasn't about to let up. When the time came for the final qualifying heat in the 200-meter dash, she took me aside.

Mae: Listen, Wilma, do you want to make the United States Olympic team?

Wilma Past: You bet I do!

Mae: Then listen to me. All you have to do in this race is stick with me. Put everything else out of your mind.

Wilma Present: I remember the gun going off, and I remember taking off with a good start. When I looked up, I saw that I had actually passed Mae and was ahead of her! She pulled up, and we finished in a dead heat, breaking the tape at the same instant!

Wilma Past: We did it! We did it!

Mae: We sure did! We're going to the Olympics! You know, Wilma, if you hadn't pulled back, you'd have beaten me in that race. I knew you had it in you, but I wondered when it would come out. Today it did.

Wilma Past: I don't think I'll ever be afraid to challenge anyone again. Thanks, Mae.

Wilma Present: When we got back to Tennessee State, people kept coming around to wish me well.

Teammate 2: Congratulations, Wilma! We're all real proud of you!

Teammate 3: Hey, Wilma, you sure put Tennessee State on the map!

Teammate 4: Just wait until the Olympics. Then the whole world will know about it!

Wilma Present: Back home in Clarksville, everyone was excited, too.

Yvonne: Wilma, you're famous! The newspaper says you're one of the fastest women in the whole world.

Mama: I can't help remembering, child, that only a couple of years ago, you were going to Nashville for treatments on your leg. Now here you are going to Australia for the Olympics!

Man: We sure are proud of you, Wilma. And we want you to go to Melbourne in style, so some of the merchants in Clarksville got together to get you this luggage and a new wardrobe to take along with our very best wishes.

Wilma Past: Thank you all, very much. I'll never forget what you've done for me.

Wilma Present: In October 1956, we flew to Melbourne, Australia. At first, I felt overwhelmed by all the people speaking different languages, but I soon realized we were all there for the same reason.

Wilma Past: You know something, Mae? For the first time in my life, I feel I'm not being judged by the color of my skin. Here, judgments depend on performance.

Mae: Well, speaking of performance, we've got to start working on ours, especially our baton-passing. There's no question about it, our timing is off.

Wilma Present: Passing the baton is one of the most important and most difficult things in running a relay. Split-second timing is an absolute necessity. In fact, a number of upsets have occurred in previous Olympic Games because of an error made during a handoff.

Wilma Past: I sure do miss Coach Temple. He'd know what we're doing wrong.

Mae: Well, we'll just have to try to remember what he taught us and keep on practicing.

Wilma Present: My very first Olympic race was three days into the games. It was the qualifying heat for the 200-meter race. I made it through the first heat, and moved on to the semifinals where only the first- and second-place runners would advance. I came in third and was eliminated. I don't know what happened, except that I didn't run as fast as I should have. I felt terrible.

Wilma Past: I can't eat or sleep. I've let everybody down. How will I ever be able to face them back home? I'm a failure.

Mae: I know how bad you feel, Wilma, but you've got another chance to show what you can do.

Wilma Past: You're right, Mae. I've just got to do well in the relay.

Wilma Present: Before the relay, Mae, as team captain, gathered us together to give us a pep talk.

Mae: Girls, I know we can do it if we give it all we've got! Let's make it into the top three and win ourselves a medal!

Wilma Past: We've got to—for Coach Temple and everyone else back home.

Wilma Present: There were teams from six countries in that relay race, and I must confess that no one was expecting much from us. Mae ran an excellent first leg keeping us tied for the lead. The second runner lost some ground to several teams before passing the baton to me. It was a clean pass and I got off well. I passed two runners on my leg, pulling us into third place. Our anchor runner held our position. We had done it! We had captured third place and bronze medals for ourselves and for the United States.

Mae: Well, I think we can go home feeling mighty proud!

Teammate 3: We sure surprised a lot of people today.

Wilma Present: I was happy that I had salvaged something out of Melbourne, and I told myself a bronze medal wasn't all that bad for a sixteen-year-old from Tennessee. But as the Olympic Games ended, I could hear the voice of Mrs. Hoskins, my fourth-grade teacher.

Mrs. Hoskins: Wilma, if you want to do something, do it. Don't daydream about it. Do it!

Wilma Present: Right then and there, I made a promise to myself.

Wilma Past: Four years from now, wherever the Olympics are held, I'm going to be there, and I'm going to win a gold medal or two for the United States!

Wilma Present: When I got home to Clarksville, I found Burt High School closed for the day so the students could attend a special assembly in my honor. When I walked out on stage, all the kids cheered and gave me flowers. After the assembly, I couldn't wait to see Coach Gray.

Coach Gray: Congratulations, Wilma! You've come a long way. How do you feel?

Wilma Past: Okay, but having to give that speech in the assembly scared me more than the Olympics! By the way, Coach, I heard there's a game tonight. I haven't played much basketball lately, but I'm in great shape. Can I play? Please?

Coach Gray: Skeeter, you haven't changed a bit! Of course you can play!

Wilma Present: A lot happened over the next few years. After high school, I entered Tennessee State University on a full athletic scholarship and joined Coach Temple's Tigerbelle track team. The 1960 Olympic trials were held the end of my sophomore year.

Coach Temple: Are you all set Wilma? The 200-meter race is next.

Wilma Past: I don't feel much like running today, Coach. But I'm ready to give it a try . . . and get it over with.

Wilma Present: I remember when the race was over, I plopped down next to Coach Temple, and he was smiling.

Coach Temple: Good race, Wilma. You're doing all right, aren't you?

Wilma Present: Later, two of my teammates came running over.

Teammate 2: Say, Wilma, why aren't you celebrating?

Wilma Past: Celebrating? What for? I mean, I'm glad I made the Olympic team, but I made it once before, you know.

Teammate 3: No, no, that's not what we mean. We're talking about your time—twenty-two point nine seconds.

Teammate 2: It's a world record!

Wilma Past: WHAT?

Teammate 3: You mean nobody told you? You just set a record for the fastest 200 meters ever run by a woman!

Wilma Present: I couldn't get over it, I'd set a world record, and I hadn't even felt like running! By the end of the trials, I'd qualified for three events—the 100 meters, the 200 meters, and the relay. Some of the other Tennessee State Tigerbelles also made the team. Best of all, Ed Temple was named coach of the United States Olympic Women's Track Team. After a three-week training session, we were off to Rome, Italy!

Wilma Past: Coach Temple, I just love Rome, and this 100 degree temperature is perfect for me. It feels just like the weather in Tennessee.

Coach Temple: You know, Wilma, it's a funny thing, but for the last two nights I've had the same dream. I keep seeing you with three Olympic gold medals around your neck.

Wilma Past: I sure do hope your dream comes true!

Wilma Present: But on the day before I was scheduled to run in my first race, disaster struck. It was a hot afternoon, and some of us were running through a sprinkler on a field of nice, soft grass.

Teammate 2: This is a great way to cool off, isn't it?

Teammate 3: Sure is, but we'd better get going. Practice starts in ten minutes, and you know how Coach Temple feels if anyone's late.

Wilma Past: Okay. Just let me run through one last time. . . . Ow!

Teammate 4: Wilma! What happened?

Wilma Past: My ankle . . . I stepped in a hole and twisted my ankle. Ow! It hurts so much!

© Macmillan/McGraw-Hill

Wilma Present: The trainer took one look and made a face; my ankle was swollen and discolored. He taped it up real tight and had me elevate it. I kept my leg up until the next morning—the day of the 100-meter final. Rumors were flying that I was out of the race. But when I put my weight on my foot, my ankle held up. I knew then I'd be able to run. That day, the stadium was jammed. For some reason, the fans had taken a liking to me, and when I walked out on the track, they started to chant.

All: Wil-ma! Wil-ma! Wil-ma!

Wilma Present: The tension was building. I put everything out of my mind and concentrated on the race I had to run. Then we were off! My start was good; I came out second or third in the field. My ankle felt all right. When I reached fifty meters, I saw that I had left them all behind—and I was just beginning to turn on the speed. By seventy meters, I knew the race was mine; nobody was going to catch me. I had won my first gold medal!

Coach Temple: That's number one, Wilma!

Wilma Past: Three days later, I ran in the 200-meter final.

All: Wil-ma! Wil-ma! Wil-ma! Go . . . go . . . go!

Coach Temple: She's way ahead. She's going to do it!

Teammate 3: Wilma did it again! She's got her second gold!

Wilma Present: That left the relay. This was my chance to become the first American woman to win three Olympic gold medals. Everybody was talking about the teams from Russia, West Germany, and Britain. Well, we beat them and set a world's record in the process! The crowd went wild.

All: Wil-ma! Wil-ma! Hooray!

Wilma Present: I had done it—the first American woman to win three gold medals. I had to share the moment with my family.

Wilma Past: Dear Folks,

Three Olympic gold medals—what a feeling! After the playing of "The Star Spangled Banner," I came away from the victory stand, and I was mobbed. People were pushing microphones into my face, pounding my back, and calling me the "Tennessee Tornado." I couldn't believe it. Finally, the American officials grabbed me and escorted me to safety. One of them told me that life would never be the same again.

Wilma Present: That official was right! I was the darling of the press, but some animosity was developing toward me on the part of the other American women runners. The jealousy grew so intense that some of the Tigerbelles—girls I had been running with for years—were turning on me.

Teammate 2: Listen to this. The paper says she has long, lissome legs and a pert charm.

Teammate 3: How nice.

Teammate 2: There's more. It says she makes all the other runners look like they're churning on a treadmill.

Teammate 4: That means us, right?

Teammate 2: No one talks about us. It's just Wilma, Wilma, Wilma. They forget that we ran the relay, too.

Wilma Present: It all came to a head—literally—in London, where our team was participating in the British Empire Games. I had to appear at a banquet, and I looked a mess.

Wilma Past: Oh, where are those hair rollers? I've got to meet Coach Temple in an hour and I look awful.

Teammate 2: Gee, Wilma, I have no idea where they are.

Teammate 4: Me, either.

Teammate 3: Don't worry, Wilma. I'm sure they'll love you anyway.

Wilma Present: When Coach Temple learned what had happened, he was furious. He called a team meeting, but as he discovered the next day, his lecture didn't have much effect. The Tigerbelles were entered in the women's relay. The stadium was packed with fans who wanted to see the fastest women's relay team in history, but my three teammates had something else in mind.

Teammate 2: Let's just take it easy today, ladies.

Teammate 3: Yeah! I'm feeling kinda tired.

Wilma Present: They loped around the track just fast enough to keep us in the race. By the time I got the baton, the leading runner was forty yards ahead of me. Well, I was determined to win that race, so I poured on the speed. I caught up with the front runner at the tape—and won! The crowd went wild. So did Coach Temple.

Coach Temple: When we get back to Tennessee State, you three are on probation!

Wilma Present: From that point on, my teammates ran their best, but they shunned me when we were off the field. It was a relief when Coach Temple announced that we were going home. We landed at the Nashville airport, and home had never looked so good.

Wilma Past: I never expected such a huge crowd, Coach.

Coach Temple: Seems like everyone in Nashville is here to greet us—the governor, the mayor, television stations, marching bands. I've never seen anything like it.

Wilma Past: It's great, Coach, but I just want to go home to my family in Clarksville.

Wilma Present: In a few days, my folks joined me in a motorcade parade down the streets of my hometown. It was the most amazing event because the whole town—black and white—turned out to greet me.

Wilma Past: Mama, do you realize this parade is the very first integrated event in Clarksville?

Mama: And you made it happen, Wilma. Why, I never thought I'd live to see this day.

Wilma Present: That night, for the first time in the history of Clarksville, black people and white people attended a banquet together. One of the featured speakers was County Judge William Hudson.

Judge: Welcome, everyone. Wilma Rudolph has competed with the world and has brought home three gold medals. Not only that, she has inspired another victory right here at home. In working together to put on this banquet in her honor, I think we've learned a worthwhile lesson: If you want to get good music out of a piano, you have to play both the white and the black keys.

Wilma Present: By the beginning of 1961, I'd completed my education, getting a degree in elementary education. I'd also received hundreds of invitations and honors. One of my proudest moments came when President Kennedy invited me, my mother, and Coach Temple to the White House. After returning from that Washington trip, I started to do some hard thinking.

Wilma Past: I'm twenty-two years old, and I've won three Olympic gold medals. So where do I go from here, Coach?

Coach Temple: What about the 1964 Olympics, Wilma?

Wilma Past: I don't know. . . . I want to have a family, and I'd like to help kids like me make it. On the other hand, it would be exciting to compete again in '64. But if I did, I'd have to win at least three more gold medals, or else people would think I'm a failure.

Coach Temple: I understand, Wilma, and remember this: If you lose in '64, that's what people will remember—the losses, not the three gold medals in 1960.

Wilma Present: I had a lot to think about. Then, in 1962, a major meet was slated with the Soviet Union. I trained hard, for in the back of my mind was the thought that this might be the right time to end my career. I wanted to retire on top, even if it meant retiring earlier than I needed to. First came the 100 meters, and I won it easily. Then came the relay, an event the Russian team excelled at. When I got the baton for the final lap, the Russian runner was about forty yards ahead of me. I started picking up speed and closing on her.

Coach Temple: That's the way, Wilma! Pour it on!

Wilma Present: She saw me coming out of the corner of her eye, and I could tell she couldn't believe that I was there. Well, I caught her, passed her, and won the race. The crowd was on its feet, giving me a standing ovation, and I knew that it was time—time to retire, with the sweet taste of victory.

Wilma Past: Whew! I thought I'd never finish signing autographs. I know I'll miss the running, but this day had to come sometime, didn't it, Coach?

Coach Temple: It comes to all of us. You're a real champ, Wilma. You've opened lots of doors for lots of people. I'll always be proud of you. Are you okay? Do you want a lift back to the hotel?

Wilma Past: I think I'd just like to sit here by myself for awhile. Thanks for everything, Coach.

Wilma Present: I was untying my track shoes, when out from the shadows came a young boy who had been pushed aside by the crowd. He was clutching a scrap of paper and a pencil.

Young Boy: Miss Rudolph . . . ?

Wilma Past: Have you been waiting all this time? Come on over and sit down by me. Do you want to be a runner, too?

Young Boy: Yes, and I dream about being in the Olympics some day. Miss Rudolph, . . . can I please have your autograph?

Wilma Past: Son, I'll do better than that.

Wilma Present: I took off my track shoes and signed my name on both of them. Then I handed them to the boy.

Wilma Past: Here, these are for you. And let me tell you what someone once told me: If you want to do something, do it. Don't daydream about it. Do it!

Samantha Smith:
Ambassador of Goodwill

by Gail Tuchman

~~~~~~~~~~~~~~~~~~~~

CAST:
Narrator
Jane Smith
Arthur Smith
Samantha Smith
Mrs. Peabody
UPI Reporter
Soviet Official
Yuri Andropov
Reporter 1
Reporter 2
Librarian
Natasha Semenikhina
Natasha Kashirina
Madame Tereshkova
Leonid Zamyatin

Narrator:	The clock in the hall had just chimed two when Jane Smith woke up with a start. Was that a cry she heard coming from her daughter's room?
Jane Smith:	Arthur! Arthur, wake up!
Arthur Smith:	Huh? . . . What's the matter, Jane? It's the middle of the night.
Jane Smith:	I know. I'm sorry, but I'm sure I heard Samantha cry out.
Arthur Smith:	You stay in bed; I'll go check. Samantha may be having a nightmare. She's been having a lot of bad dreams lately.
Narrator:	Samantha's father quickly got up and walked down the hall to his daughter's room. He found a half-asleep Samantha with her head buried under her pillow.
Arthur Smith:	Samantha, it's Dad. Is everything all right?
Samantha:	Huh?
Arthur Smith:	Is everything all right? Mom thought she heard you cry out.
Samantha:	I think I was having a dream . . . another terrible dream. Bombs were falling and I was lost. I couldn't find you or Mom.
Arthur Smith:	Well, we're here, honey. Everything is all right. You were just having a bad dream. Now, close your eyes and go back to sleep.
Samantha:	Night, Dad.
Narrator:	Arthur Smith waited a few minutes until Samantha had dropped back to sleep. Then he quietly tiptoed out of the room. Down the hall, his wife was sitting up waiting for him.
Jane Smith:	Was it another bad dream, Arthur?

Arthur Smith: Yes, it was. Given what's been in the news lately, it's no wonder that Samantha's having nightmares. Maybe it would be a good idea to spend a little time tomorrow talking about what's going on—and how it makes her feel.

Narrator: There was no doubt about it. In 1982, tensions between the United States and the Soviet Union were running high. It was a time when the door was officially closed to cultural, educational, and athletic exchanges between the two nations. It was a time when American dollars and Russian rubles were being poured into the build-up of military bases and stockpiles of missiles and nuclear weapons. And it was a time of confusion and concern for many young people. Samantha Reed Smith of Manchester, Maine, was no exception. The next morning at breakfast, Mrs. Smith talked with Samantha about her dream.

Samantha: It was awful! Is there going to be a war, Mom? I keep seeing programs on TV about missiles and nuclear bombs. Scientists on a show last night said nuclear war would wreck the earth and destroy our atmosphere!

Jane Smith: No wonder you had a nightmare!

Samantha: All that talk about war really scares me. What I don't understand is why anyone would start a war. I don't want my whole future destroyed!

Jane Smith: Neither do I, honey. But this is a heavy subject to discuss on an empty stomach. Why don't you have your breakfast first, and then we'll talk about it? While you eat, I'll look for a magazine that has an article I think you'd be interested in.

Narrator: Samantha sipped her orange juice and downed her oatmeal and toast as her mom rummaged through a pile of magazines.

Jane Smith: Here's the magazine I was looking for—it's got a photo of the new Soviet leader, Yuri Andropov, on the cover. The feature story is about relations between the United States and the Soviet Union. The point of the article is that people in both countries share exactly the same fear.

Samantha: What fear is that?

Jane Smith: The fear that the other country will launch a nuclear strike.

Samantha: Well, if everyone is afraid of a nuclear attack, why would anyone press the button to blow up the world? I don't get it. That seems so dumb to me! From what Granddad told me about World War II, I didn't think anyone would ever want to have another war. Mom, you should write to Mr. Andropov to find out what's causing this mess with Russia.

Jane Smith: You know, that's quite an idea, Samantha. Why don't you write to him?

Samantha: Come on, Mom, you do it. You'll know just what to say. Besides, a world leader's not going to listen to a kid.

Jane Smith: I'm not so sure about that. It's because you're a kid that you have a great concern about the future of the world. I think world leaders would want to hear what young people have to say. You're a good writer—give it a try.

Samantha: Well . . . I guess it couldn't hurt. It's hard to tell much about Mr. Andropov from this picture, but maybe I'll get to know him better if I write to him and he writes back.

Narrator: Samantha picked up a pencil and began drafting her letter to Yuri Andropov, head of the Union of Soviet Socialist Republics. At dinner that night, she brought her letter to the table.

Samantha: It's finally finished. I tried to use my best penmanship so Mr. Andropov wouldn't have any trouble reading it! Would you listen to it just to be sure it all makes sense?

Arthur Smith: Sure, Samantha. Go ahead, we're listening.

Dear Mr. Andropov,

My name is Samantha Smith. I am ten years old. Congratulations on your new job. I have been worrying about Russia and the United States getting into a nuclear war. Are you going to vote to have a war or not? If you aren't please tell me how you are going to help to not have a war. This question you do not have to answer, but I would like to know why you want to conquer the world or at least our country. God made the world for us to live together in peace and not to fight.

Sincerely,
Samantha Smith

Jane Smith: That's a great letter, Samantha! You've asked the kind of thoughtful questions that every world leader needs to think about.

Narrator: The letter was mailed, and nearly four months passed without any response. Samantha had put the whole thing out of her mind—almost. But one day in April, Mrs. Peabody, the secretary at the Manchester Elementary School, excitedly asked that Samantha be excused from class.

Samantha: What's wrong, Mrs. Peabody? Did my mother call to tell you my dentist appointment's been changed?

Mrs. Peabody: No, Samantha. This has nothing to do with a dentist appointment! A reporter from United Press International wants to speak with you.

Samantha: What? Why me?

Mrs. Peabody: Did you write to the Soviet leader, Mr. Andropov?

Samantha: Andropov? . . . Well, yes I did. But that was so long ago, I've almost forgotten what I said in my letter!

Mrs. Peabody: Well, try to remember! I left the reporter hanging on the other end of the telephone while I ran to get you. Go ahead and pick up the phone in the principal's office.

Samantha: Hello. This is Samantha Smith.

UPI Reporter: Hello, Samantha. I'm a reporter from UPI. Is it true that you wrote a letter to Yuri Andropov?

Samantha: Yes, it's true. But how did you find out about it?

UPI Reporter: There was an article about your letter in *Pravda*, the Russian newspaper. They even printed a picture of it, but the story didn't say whether Mr. Andropov is planning to write back to you. Do you think he will?

Samantha: Well, I don't know, but I hope he does!

UPI Reporter: Look, I'll give the school my number so you can reach me if you hear anything more from Mr. Andropov. That way we can keep in touch. Okay?

Samantha: Okay. Thanks for letting me know about my letter. It was nice talking to you. Bye.

Narrator: That afternoon, Samantha's dad obtained a copy of *Pravda*. He taught at the University of Maine, so he asked a colleague in the Russian department to translate the article for him. When Mr. Smith got home, he showed the translation to Samantha and her mother.

Arthur Smith: Well, the article doesn't answer any of your questions, Samantha, and it doesn't say anything about why Mr. Andropov hasn't responded to your letter. What it does say is that you should be "excused for misunderstanding" because you are "only ten years old."

Samantha: Misunderstanding! Only ten years old! That's so insulting! I'm going to write another letter to find out what's going on. Who should I send it to this time?

Jane Smith: Well, you might start with the Soviet ambassador to the United States.

Samantha: Who's that?

Arthur Smith: Ambassador Dobrynin. He's the head of the Soviet embassy in Washington, D.C.

Samantha: Okay. I'll ask Ambassador Dobrynin if Mr. Andropov is going to answer my questions. Then I'll tell him they're good ones, and it shouldn't matter if I'm ten years old!

Narrator: A week later, Samantha received a telephone call from a man with a heavy accent. She had to listen hard in order to understand him.

Official: Dobree dyen, Samantha Smith, I'm calling from the Soviet embassy. This is to inform you that you will soon receive a reply from Yuri Andropov, the general secretary of the Central Committee of the Communist Party of the USSR.

Samantha: You're not one of Dad's friends playing a joke, are you?

Official: Nyet! This is not a joke. I want you to call me when the letter arrives. Write down these telephone numbers. Then call me when Chairman Andropov's letter arrives. Do you understand?

Samantha: Yes, I think so!

Narrator: Samantha's dad checked the telephone numbers, and sure enough, they were for the Soviet embassy in Washington, D.C.! Then, on the morning of April 26, 1983, just as Samantha was leaving for school, she got a call from Alice, the postmistress in Manchester, saying that a very official-looking envelope had arrived. Samantha and Mr. Smith rushed to the post office, opened the envelope, and pulled out three pages of heavy, cream-colored stationery. The letter was typed in Russian, but an English translation was attached.

Yuri Andropov: Dear Samantha,

I received your letter, which is like many others that have reached me recently from your country and from other countries around the world.

It seems to me—I can tell by your letter—that you are a courageous and honest girl, resembling Becky, the friend of Tom Sawyer in the famous book of your compatriot Mark Twain. This book is well known and loved in our country by all boys and girls.

Samantha: Imagine that! The Russian leader is comparing me to Becky Thatcher! I think Mr. Andropov is trying to be friendly.

Yuri Andropov: You write that you are anxious about whether there will be a nuclear war between our two countries. And you ask are we doing anything so that war will not break out. Your question is the most important of those that every thinking man can pose. I will reply to you seriously and honestly.

Arthur Smith: Well, it sounds as if Mr. Andropov is taking you seriously—even though you're "only ten years old"!

Narrator: The letter went on to say that the Soviet Union was doing everything it could to prevent war because all citizens of the USSR remembered the devastating effects of World War II, when millions of Soviets were killed. He also said that the Soviets want to live in peace with all other nations, and that the Soviet Union would never use nuclear weapons first against any country. The letter continued.

Yuri Andropov: It seems to me that this is a sufficient answer to your second question: "Why do you want to wage war against the whole world or at least the United States?" We want nothing of the kind. No one in our country—neither workers, peasants, writers nor doctors, neither grown-ups nor children, nor members of the government—wants either a big or "little" war.

Samantha: That's just what Mom told me that magazine article on Andropov said—that people in Russia don't want war any more than we do.

Yuri Andropov: We want peace—there is something that we are occupied with: growing wheat, building and inventing, writing books and flying into space. We want peace for ourselves and for all peoples of the planet. For our children and for you, Samantha.

Arthur Smith: Read what he says next! Samantha, you're not going to believe this part!

Yuri Andropov: I invite you, if your parents will let you, to come to our country, the best time being the summer. You will find out about our country, meet with your contemporaries, visit an international children's camp—Artek—on the sea. And see for yourself: in the Soviet Union—everyone is for peace and friendship among peoples. Thank you for your letter. I wish you all the best in your young life.

Y. Andropov

Samantha: Mr. Andropov wants me to visit the Soviet Union! I think I'm in shock. Daddy, can we go?

Arthur Smith: We'll see, Samantha. We'll talk about it after you get home from school. I think I'm in a state of shock, too! Visit the Soviet Union as a guest of Mr. Andropov. . . . The whole thing is incredible!

Narrator: Swarms of reporters and TV newscasters were gathered on the front lawn when Samantha returned home from school that afternoon. They besieged her with questions.

Reporter 1: Why did you write to Mr. Andropov?

Reporter 2: Did you expect Mr. Andropov to answer your letter?

Reporter 1: Will you go to the Soviet Union?

Reporter 2: What do you think of all this?

Samantha: I'm not used to all this, but I'll try to answer your questions one at a time. It's going to be weird seeing myself on TV!

Narrator: But Samantha quickly got used to being in the limelight. TV and radio news shows began calling from all over the country and even from around the world. Two television networks sent a chartered plane to fly Samantha and her mom to New York City for appearances on "Nightline," "CBS Morning News," and the "Today Show." A short time later, Johnny Carson invited Samantha to be a guest on the "Tonight Show," and the family flew out to California.

Arthur Smith: I never really expected Mr. Andropov to answer your letter, and now here we are in a media blitz!

Samantha: I can't believe it, either. Look at all these letters—I've gotten hundreds of them from all over the world! And the phone rings every two minutes all day long!

Narrator: However, mixed with outpourings of admiration for Samantha was some genuine skepticism about Mr. Andropov's motives. Some Americans criticized his letter as "propaganda" and "clever public relations" for the Soviet Union. Others said he was "taking advantage of a ten-year-old's innocence." Ronald Reagan, who was then president of the United States, did not publicly acknowledge either Samantha's letter or Andropov's answer. Given the strong feelings that surfaced on both sides of the issue, Samantha's family was faced with making a difficult decision about visiting the Soviet Union. One night, Arthur and Jane Smith sat up talking long after Samantha had gone to bed.

Arthur Smith: It's hard to know what to do, Jane—not only because of the political implications, but also because of Samantha. The spotlight of the world will be on her if we make this trip. Do you think she'll be able to handle the pressure? Is it fair to put her in this position?

Jane Smith: I've been thinking about that, too. It's asking a lot of a child who was so shy that she wouldn't even try out for the school play. I'm not sure what we should do.

Arthur Smith: On the other hand, Samantha seems committed to going. I think she really believes that she can make a difference to world peace.

Jane Smith: Yes, she does. You know, maybe we've just got to have faith that Samantha will come through.

Arthur Smith: I guess that's the key, Jane. . . . And I keep thinking that it would be a shame to deprive her of such an incredible experience.

Jane Smith: I think we should accept the invitation. We could go during your vacation in July.

Arthur Smith: All right, Jane. Let's tell Samantha first thing tomorrow. She's finding it very difficult to think or talk about anything else, and I think we're both getting tired of saying, "We'll see!"

Narrator: The next morning, Jane and Arthur Smith told an excited Samantha they'd be making the trip. They spent the next few hours talking about it, with Samantha asking all sorts of questions about the Soviet Union.

Jane Smith: You know, it would be a good idea if you went over to the library to do a little research. How about it, Samantha?

Samantha: Can't you just tell me about Russia? It'll take forever to do all that reading!

Arthur Smith: At this point, we don't know that much more than you do! We're all going to have to do some reading before we leave, and we're counting on you to share what you learn with us! Besides, by reading and looking at pictures now, we'll recognize some of the famous monuments and buildings when we actually see them this summer.

Samantha: Okay. Maybe I'll check out a few books—but not now. I've got a few phone calls to make before I do anything. My friends just aren't going to believe that we're actually going.

Narrator: Later that week, Samantha headed over to the library, where she asked the librarian for help in finding books on Russian history and for travel guides to the Soviet Union.

Librarian: The travel books are over on the shelf by the window, Samantha.

Samantha: Thanks, Mrs. DeMicco. I found one book that said that Russia is really called the "Soviet Union" and the people are called "Soviets" because there are many parts of the country that are not Russian.

Librarian: That's true. But Russian is the official language of the Soviet Union.

Samantha: Maybe I can learn to speak a little Russian. The country looks beautiful in these photos. I always pictured the Soviet Union as sort of dark and gray, but the buildings have lots of gold. It all looks so different from Maine.

Librarian: It certainly does.

Narrator: After checking out some books, Samantha stuffed them into her backpack and headed home.

Jane Smith: How'd you make out at the library?

Samantha: Okay, I guess. I looked through a lot of books.

Jane Smith: What were your impressions?

Samantha: Well, when I looked at pictures of Soviet people, I began to wonder if I can be friends with Soviet kids. Will they think that I'm a spy or that I'm afraid of them or that I want to conquer them? Maybe they'll hate me!

Jane Smith: It's understandable that you feel that way, Samantha. But do you remember how many kids wrote to you saying that you were very brave to send that letter?

Samantha: Well, writing the letter didn't take any bravery, but I will have to be brave if the Soviet kids don't like me, that's for sure.

Narrator: People 'round the world watched and waited as Samantha and her parents began the first leg of their historic journey from Maine to Moscow. At the Montreal airport, where they were about to board a Soviet airliner, Samantha was mobbed by a crowd of reporters pushing microphones at her and shouting out questions. Everything got so crazy that Samantha bit one of the microphones that was pushed into her face! Then she was whisked onto the plane.

Samantha: Now that I think of it, that scene in the Montreal airport was pretty funny. If the reporters had just stood still and raised their hands, I wouldn't have panicked. But then, it wouldn't have been as exciting either!

Narrator: Nine hours later, the Smith family landed at the airport in Moscow, the sixth-largest city in the world. This airport was as crowded and noisy with reporters as the one in Canada. People from the Soviet Friendship Society welcomed Samantha and her parents with flowers.

Natasha S.: How do you do, Samantha Smith. I'm Natasha Semenikhina. I will be your guide during your stay in our country. First, I'll take you to Hotel Sovietskaya, where you can relax a little, and later we'll have dinner.

Samantha: It's nice to meet you and to be in your country. I feel like I'm dreaming. It's so incredible to be here!

Narrator: The family arrived at the Sovietskaya, which Samantha thought looked more like a palace than a hotel. After a short rest, Natasha took them into a huge dining room, where Samantha scrutinized the menu.

Samantha: I think I'll try the chicken Kiev. What is it?

Natasha S.: Well, this dish is named after Kiev, a famous city in the Soviet Union.

Samantha: Actually, what I meant is, how is it made?

Natasha S.: Oh, it's a piece of rolled chicken prepared with hot butter in the center. I'll show you how to cut it so the butter won't squirt you!

Samantha: Thanks, that sounds delicious. I'm going to order chicken Kiev for the rest of the trip!

Narrator: The next day, with police cars leading the way, the car carrying the Smiths and their guide roared through the streets of Moscow to Red Square— site of some of the most famous landmarks in all of the Soviet Union.

Samantha: Look! See all those people waiting in line? I'll bet that's Lenin's tomb.

Natasha S.: Samantha, I am impressed. Do you know who Lenin was?

Samantha: Sure. He was a famous leader in the Russian Revolution in 1917. See, Mom, I do remember some of the stuff from those library books!

Narrator: Because of their special status, the Smiths were able to bypass the long lines. After visiting Lenin's tomb, they took flowers to Yuri Gargarin's tomb in tribute to the first man in space.

Natasha S.: Our next stop will be the Kremlin.

Samantha: Natasha, I know I read what kremlin means, but I can't remember it.

Natasha S.: Good, Samantha, now I will be able to justify my services as your guide for today! Kremlin means "fortress." The walled-in area of old Moscow that serves as the government center is called the Kremlin. The compound is used for other ceremonies and businesses, as well.

Narrator: They walked behind the high walls of the Kremlin to visit the old churches and ancient palaces filled with beautiful paintings and golden treasures.

Natasha S.: Now I want to show you the gigantic chandeliers in the Great Kremlin Palace.

Samantha: Each chandelier is nearly as big as our whole living room!

Natasha S.: Do you know the secret of finding out if there's real crystal in a chandelier? Stand right underneath the chandelier, look up at it, and roll your head in a circle twenty times. If you feel dizzy, that means you're standing under real crystal.

Samantha: Somehow I'm not so sure I believe that!

Narrator: The next morning, the family flew hundreds of miles south to the warm and sunny region known as the Crimea, on the Black Sea. Samantha was especially looking forward to this part of their trip—a few days at the summer camp in Artek.

Natasha S.: I think you'll like the Pioneer camp. The Pioneers are like the Scouts in your country. About 4,000 young people from all over the Soviet Union attend this camp.

Samantha: I hear that to get into Artek, you have to have super grades and be really talented in music or be a genius in science or a sports star or know a zillion different languages. I hope I'll fit in 'cause I'm really not that special in anything!

Natasha S.: I know you'll fit in just fine. Look out of the window—that welcoming committee of Pioneers lining the runway is for you!

Samantha: My goodness, there must be a thousand of them! Just look at all the flowers they have! Are they shouting my name? It sounds like they're saying "Sa-manta! Samanta!"

Natasha S.: You have good ears, Samantha. You see, there's no *th* sound in Russian. That's why they're saying "Samanta."

Narrator: As Samantha walked down the steps of the plane, a band began to play. Then, the children, dressed in Pioneer uniforms, sang songs of welcome, after which some dancers brought her a round loaf of bread with a bowl of salt sitting on top.

Natasha S.: They're giving you the traditional welcome of bread and salt.

Samantha: Am I supposed to eat it or not?

Natasha S.: As a sign that you've accepted their friendship, break some bread and dip it in the salt.

Samantha: Mmm . . . it's delicious!

Natasha S.: The director wants to know if you'd like to stay with your parents or with the Pioneer girls.

Samantha: With the Pioneers—absolutely!

Narrator: A place had been made ready for Samantha in the Sea Camp dormitory because the campers in that section knew a little English. Olga, the section leader, took Samantha to meet her roommates.

Natasha K.: Dobree dyen, Samantha. I'm Natasha Kashirina, one of the girls in your room. There are ten of us altogether. This is Vera, Svieta, Illona, and Vasilina. You'll meet the others soon.

Samantha: Dobree dyen, Natasha! You speak English very well.

Natasha K.: Thank you. My mother teaches English at a school in Leningrad.

Narrator: Within a few minutes, Samantha and Natasha had become friends.

Natasha K.: If you look out past the balcony, you can see the rocky beach and smell the Black Sea.

Samantha: It's not really black, and it's not that different from the Atlantic Ocean, is it? The only difference I can see is that there are no really big waves.

Natasha K.: The other difference that you can't see is that it's extremely salty, which makes it easy to float. In fact, you'll almost feel as if you're wearing a life jacket when you swim.

Samantha: Sort of like the Great Salt Lake in Utah! For some reason, I thought Artek would be more rustic— with tents and canoes like a nature camp—but it isn't at all. I can't believe the beautiful gardens. Everything is so elegant!

Natasha K.: Speaking of elegant, this Artek Pioneer uniform is for you. After you put it on, I'll tie your hair up with one of these white chiffon bows that we like to wear. And here's a blue and white scarf for around your neck to show you're a visitor.

Narrator: When it was time for bed, all the girls stayed up very late, talking and whispering.

Samantha: I feel right at, home, Natasha, because everyone is so friendly. It's like a big slumber party back in Maine.

Narrator: On the second day at Sea Camp, many of the Pioneers wrote out wishes for the future. They put their wishes in bottles and sealed them with corks and wax. Then they took an Artek boat out on the Black Sea and threw the bottles into the deep water.

Samantha: It's just like a gigantic wishing well!

Natasha K.: What did you wish for?

Samantha: Peace and friendship.

Natasha K.: I wished for peace, too!

Narrator: There was a band on the boat, and all the kids linked arms and rocked back and forth and sang. Samantha sang a little in Russian, too. The next few days at Artek were busy ones, for the campers were planning end-of-session activities. When the last night of camp finally came, there was a gala celebration of parades, fireworks, dancing, and costume shows. Sadly, Samantha said good-bye to all the new friends she had made. She and

Natasha Kashirina promised to write to each other often. Then it was time for the Smiths to fly off to their last major stop on the trip—the city of Leningrad.

Narrator: As the family took their seats inside the beautiful blue and gold auditorium, the lights dimmed, and Samantha watched the first act of the ballet, mesmerized.

Natasha S.: We have a special treat here in Leningrad. Tonight we attend a performance of the world-famous Kirov Ballet.

Samantha: I took ballet lessons when I was little, but this is the first time I've ever seen a real ballet. I thought it would be boring, but it's terrific! The prima ballerina, Alia Cizova, is unbelievable. How does she jump so high and turn so fast?

Natasha S.: You'll have a chance to ask her those questions yourself, Samantha. A guide is going to take you backstage during this intermission.

Narrator: Following a whirlwind backstage visit, Samantha rushed back to her seat just as the lights dimmed for the next act.

Samantha: [whispering] You won't believe this! Alia Cizova came up to me backstage and presented me with a pair of her toe shoes. She even autographed them. I can't wait to try them on!

Jane Smith: [whispering] Shh! Not now, Samantha. Sit still and watch the ballet; you can try on the toe shoes later.

Narrator: Samantha moved over to sit with Natasha after the next act.

Natasha S.: Now you can sneak your toe shoes on! Don't forget to tie the ribbons around your ankles.

Samantha: They fit! Alia Cizova and I are the same size! It's a good thing I have big feet for my age!

Narrator: After their visit to the ballet in Leningrad, the Smiths took the midnight sleeper train, the Red Arrow Express, back to Moscow. The following day, they were received at the Soviet Women's Committee for a luncheon with its director. Samantha learned that this woman, Madame Tereshkova, had made history in 1963 as the first woman in space.

Mme. Tereshkova: I kiss you, Samantha! I kiss you! And I hug you to pieces! It's so dangerous to have our countries afraid of each other and spending so much money on war equipment. I hope our countries can be friends once again and spend our time and money on peaceful activities. Friendship is very important.

Samantha: You were the first woman cosmonaut, Madame Tereshkova, and I hope someday you'll be the first woman president of the Soviet Union!

Narrator: A whirlwind of activity followed. At the Olympic Center, Samantha tried riding a racing bicycle, but it was far too big for her, so expert cyclists rode beside her—just in case. She got a lesson on twirling ribbons from champion Soviet gymnasts, went to the Moscow Circus, the Moscow Puppet Theater, and then to a wonderful toy museum. Samantha knew her trip was coming to an end.

Samantha: Mom, I can't believe our trip is almost over. Do you think we'll get to meet Yuri Andropov?

Jane Smith: Natasha said that the Soviet officials would let her know today. You know, Mr. Andropov has been out of the public eye lately because of poor health, but I'm still hoping we can meet him.

Narrator: Later that day, Natasha had disappointing news for the Smiths.

Natasha S.: I just found out that Mr. Andropov will not be able to see you. He very much regrets this, but he will send his deputy and some other Kremlin officials to meet with you in his place.

Narrator: The Kremlin deputy, whose name was Leonid Zamyatin, had white hair and looked like an American businessman. Even though he and his colleagues seemed somewhat formal to Samantha, she thought they were all very nice. The Russians and the Americans communicated through a translator.

Mr. Zamyatin: Samantha, Mr. Andropov sends his apologies for not being able to be here himself.

Samantha: Please tell Mr. Andropov that I understand, Mr. Zamyatin. I just wanted to tell him that our countries need to be friends.

Mr. Zamyatin: Your trip might help that come true, Samantha. Mr. Andropov asked me to present you with these gifts. It is his hope that this Russian samovar and this lacquered wooden box, called a palech, will remind you of your stay in the Soviet Union.

Samantha: I could never forget the last two weeks! Oh look! The box, I mean palech, has a picture of Red Square on top! Every time I look at it, I will think of our visit to Moscow!

Jane Smith: The gifts are very beautiful and thoughtful. Please thank Mr. Andropov for us.

Samantha: We have a gift for Mr. Andropov, too! It's a book by a famous American writer.

Mr. Zamyatin: Let me see . . . the title is *Mark Twain Speaking*, is it not?

Mr. Zamyatin: Thank you. I will give your special gift to Mr. Andropov.

Narrator: They all sat down to tea and talked about the concerns Samantha had expressed in her letter. After a while, everyone shook hands and said their good-byes; Mr. Zamyatin and the officers departed.

Samantha: Right. You see, we thought Mr. Andropov might like it because he has to give so many speeches himself. Besides, I know that Mr. Andropov likes Mr. Twain's stories because he told me so in the letter that he wrote to me!

Samantha: That was a good meeting! But something funny happened, and I tried hard to keep myself from laughing. Did you notice that one of the waiters was so nervous that the teacups rattled like crazy when he carried them to the table? And I noticed something else, too. A couple of times Mr. Zamyatin interrupted the translator and changed the words, so I suspect that he knows English!

Narrator: The next morning, Samantha held her last press conference in Moscow before the Smiths headed out to the airport. There they said their final good-byes to their new friends.

Natasha S.: Samantha, it is hard to say good-bye to you. I wonder, did you discover anything about the Soviet people during your visit to our country?

Samantha: Oh, Natasha, it is hard to say good-bye to you, too. I hope you'll come to visit us in Maine. And as to what I discovered, I think more than anything, I learned that the Soviet people don't want war at all. They want peace just like Americans do. Dasveedahnya, dasveedahnya! I will miss you all so much!

Narrator: The family flew from the Moscow airport back to Maine, making several stops once they reached North America. At each stopover, they were greeted by reporters, camera crews, and cheering crowds. For once, Samantha had very little to say; she was exhausted from the long trip across the Atlantic. The day after arriving home, Samantha got to ride in a convertible as the honored guest at the Manchester Festival in Maine. Banners and bands welcomed the Ambassador of Goodwill home. As always, there were reporters everywhere waiting for an opportunity to talk with her.

Reporter 1: How does it feel to be back, Samantha?

Samantha: I think Maine is a good place to come home to.

Reporter 2: Can you tell us what effect your trip had on you, Samantha?

Samantha: It's hard to believe how much my life was changed by writing that letter. Somehow, the world doesn't seem quite as scary or complicated as it did before my trip. The people of the world seem more like people in my own neighborhood. I think we're more alike than we are different. I guess that's the most important change inside me.

Narrator: The Ambassador of Goodwill returned to school, softball, and field hockey. She went back to raising Kim, her Chesapeake Bay retriever, and her cats, Phoebe and Muffin. She continued socializing with her friends and listening to rock music. But Samantha did something else, as well. She made trips and appearances on TV news and talk shows and at conferences to speak out on behalf of international cooperation and understanding. And when she did so, reporters always bombarded her with questions.

Reporter 1: What advice would you give to kids who want to get involved in politics?

Samantha: I would tell them to write a letter to whoever is president at the time, and tell him or her what you think. Hopefully, the president will realize what you think is worth listening to. If all kids did it, that'd be great.

Reporter 2: How do you think the United States and the Soviet Union benefitted from your trip?

Samantha: Well, maybe I was able to help people think about world problems in a new way. I don't want people to give up hope. I think I showed that you shouldn't be afraid of your ideas or worry just because no one else has tried something before. Go ahead and do it.

UPI Reporter: Some Americans have accused the Soviets of "using" you for propaganda. Do you agree?

Samantha: When I was interviewed on the "Today Show" right after I got Mr. Andropov's letter, I was asked if I knew what "propaganda" meant. I had no idea then, but now I do! I think the Soviets were using me, but it was propaganda for peace—they weren't using me as a reason for starting a war!

Reporter 1: Do you think it's possible to achieve world peace?

Samantha: I think there's a way we can have peace among children. As for adults—I think it's possible. But, as a kid, it's pretty hard to do something about it. I think we can achieve peace if everyone tries hard enough.

Reporter 2: Do you have any specific ideas for achieving world peace?

Samantha: I feel one way to stop the possibility of war would be to have world leaders participate in a grandchild exchange. These leaders would send their grandchildren to live with families of leaders in other nations. If we start with this kind of exchange and keep expanding it and expanding it, then all of us could look around and see only friends—no opposing nations, no enemies, and no bombs!

EPILOGUE

Narrator: In 1984, Samantha hosted a TV special in which she interviewed Democratic presidential candidates. She also appeared in the TV series "Charles in Charge" and "Lime Street." When she was returning home from London after working on the fourth episode of "Lime Street," tragedy struck. On the foggy and rainy night of August 25, 1985, Samantha Smith, aged thirteen, and her father, Arthur, were killed in an airplane crash half a mile from the Lewiston-Auburn Airport in Maine. Sympathy letters to Jane Smith poured in from around the world. Among them were condolences from the leaders of the world's two most powerful nations—the United States and the Soviet Union—for whom Samantha had left open the door to world peace. President Reagan had this to say in a telegram to Jane Smith. . . .

Pres. Reagan: Perhaps you can take some measure of comfort in the knowledge that millions of Americans, indeed millions of people, share the burdens of your grief. They also will cherish and remember Samantha, her smile, her idealism, and unaffected sweetness of spirit.

Narrator: Mr. Gorbachev, who had taken Yuri Andropov's place as head of the Soviet Union, shared similar sentiments with Mrs. Smith. . .

Mr. Gorbachev: Everyone in the Soviet Union who has known Samantha Smith will remember forever the image of the American girl who, like millions of Soviet young men and women, dreamt about peace, and about friendship between the peoples of the United States and the Soviet Union.

Narrator: To honor Samantha, the Soviet Union issued a commemorative stamp with her picture. In Maine, Samantha's home state, a bronze statue of Samantha setting free a dove—a traditional symbol of peace—was dedicated. On the memorial plaque are the following words: "Samantha Reed Smith, June 29, 1972—August 25, 1985, Maine's young ambassador of goodwill."

Jane Smith: My daughter Samantha's dream for world peace continues to live through the work of the Samantha Smith Foundation, which I established soon after her death. Each summer, a growing number of young people have participated in the Soviet/American Youth Camp exchange— with over twenty-five camps hosting the Soviet delegation during their stay in the United States. In 1991, Samantha's close friend from Artek, Natasha Kashirina, and her Pioneer leader, Olga Volkova, became involved in the exchange as camp counselors at the Worldpeace Camp in Maine. Through this program, young people from around the world achieve a better understanding of one another. This is a first step toward peace—a step toward fulfilling Samantha's dream.

A Steel Drivin' Man

by Alice Benjamin Boyton

CAST:

Narrator 1
Narrator 2
Chorus
Poppa
Granddaddy
Mama

John Henry
Joe
Pilot
Captain
Foreman
Li'l Bill
Workman 1

Workman 2
Polly Ann
Workman 3
Cap'n Tommy
Salesman
Judge

© Macmillan/McGraw-Hill

Narrator 1: The American people have been singing their songs for over two hundred years. In fact, you could say that America grew up singing. As loggers set to work clearing the land, they sang songs to the beat of their axes. Then, resting in the glow of a flickering campfire, they'd pass the time making up fanciful stories about other lumbermen—larger than life characters like Paul Bunyan, who could do a month's work in a single day. Wishful thinking, you might say!

Narrator 2: Workers in other occupations had their own heroes, too. You may have heard of Pecos Bill and Slue-Foot Sue, both Texas cowhands; Febold Feboldson, weather scientist extraordinaire from Nebraska; Joe Magarac, a Pittsburgh steelmaker; and Kemp Morgan, an oil driller from Oklahoma. These characters from folk song and story tell us a lot about life in early America, and the hard work that it took to help our young nation grow. Those who labored building the railroads that crisscrossed this country also had their own folk hero. Now gather 'round and listen to our story of a man who hammered his way into legend.

Chorus: This story's about a mighty hero,
And John Henry was his name,
You won't find him mentioned in your
   history books,
But he was a hero just the same, same, same,
But he was a hero just the same.
Some people say he came from Texas,
Some people say he came from Maine,
The fact is that he was a Louisiana man,
Born hearing the whistle of a train, train, train,
Born hearing the whistle of a train.

Narrator 1: John Henry was born around the time of the Civil War. It was an age of science and inventions; new machines were beginning to help do the work of building this country. Sometimes men and women found themselves pitted against these machines in a test of strength . . . but that's jumping ahead in our story. Let's go back and start at the beginning of John Henry's life.

Narrator 2: From the day John Henry was born, it was clear that he was someone special. That afternoon, there was a rainbow in the sky—but that wasn't all. The Mississippi River stopped in its bed and started flowing backward. And when night fell, what a night it turned out to be!

Poppa: Come on out here, Granddaddy. I never did see a night like this in all my born days, and most likely I'll never see one like it again. Will you look at that moon! It's red—as red as the blood of a hero.

Granddaddy: Not gonna be seein' it for long, son. That big black cloud rushing over is gonna cover up that moon just like a blanket. How about that! My, my, it's as dark as the inside of a cave.

Poppa: Look there, Granddaddy! Did you see that lightning? It looked like a mighty hammer whopping the earth.

Narrator 1: At that very moment, John Henry was born. A split second later, the cloud had moved on, and the moon shone, round and white as always. The stars stopped their dancing and were content just to twinkle. The river turned around and headed on down to the sea once more.

Narrator 2: In the moonlight, John Henry's daddy and granddaddy could see a stranger dressed in black riding by on an old gray mule. He stopped for just a moment as he passed the cabin, and then moved on. Everything was quiet again, except for the plaintive whistle of a train in the distance—followed by the crying of a baby.

Mama: Well, Poppa, we got us a fine, strapping boy. Just look at those arms and shoulders. I thought we might call him John Henry.

Poppa: Yup, that name suits him just fine. He surely is a big boy, Mama. Why, John Henry must weigh thirty-five pounds, at least.

Mama: Seems so, and I do declare this child's a-growin' before my very eyes. I don't know that we've got a bottle big enough to feed him with.

John Henry: Oh, don't bother with a bottle, Mama. That's for babies.

Granddaddy: John Henry, are you talking already? How about that! Well then, young fella, suppose you just tell us what you'd like to eat.

John Henry: Well, Granddaddy, if it wouldn't be too much trouble, I could do with fifty-five slices of razorback ham with red gravy and sweet potatoes piled high around them . . . and about five pots of turnip greens . . . and maybe three kettles of hominy grits, fourteen or so fried catfish, and four dozen buttermilk biscuits with maple syrup for sweetening. I've got a craving in my heart, and I'm powerful hungry, besides.

Poppa: Well, well, it sure enough looks like we've got us a bragful boy, one whose eyes are way bigger than his stomach.

Mama: Supposin' we get all the food together just this one time, Poppa. When John Henry sees he can't eat it all, maybe he'll learn his lesson.

Chorus: They set up seven wooden tables,
All the neighbors lent a hand,
There were cabbages and turnips, also black-eyed peas,

"Well, thanks," said John Henry, "This is grand, grand, grand!"

"Well, thanks," said John Henry, "This is grand!"

Granddaddy: My, my, would you look at that boy eat! I reckon he'll be full by the time he's cleared off the second table, though.

Poppa: He sure does enjoy his food, and he doesn't seem to be slowin' down, not one teeny bit!

Mama: I do declare, he's eating every last morsel!

John Henry: Course, I am. I told you I was hungry.

Mama: We thought you were just being bragful, son.

John Henry: No, Mama. I'm a natural boy. I say what I mean, and I mean what I say. I've still got that craving in my heart, but at least I'm not hungry anymore. Thanks for that mighty fine meal.

Narrator 1: So you see, it was the grown-up folks who learned a lesson, and they never again doubted John Henry. As the weeks went by, John Henry grew fast. So did his strength. One day, when he was about six weeks old, he picked up a piece of steel and his daddy's five-pound hammer.

Granddaddy: Will you listen to that hammer ringing on that steel! My, my, sounds just like the big bell in the meetinghouse.

Poppa: He sure can swing that hammer. Why, when he whops it down on a rock, the rock breaks clean in two!

John Henry: You know, Poppa, I can lift an ax, and I can pull a hoe, but nothing feels as natural as this hammer in my hand. It's a mighty peculiar thing, but when I swing this hammer and make the steel ring, I don't have that craving in my heart anymore. No sir, I feel happy.

Poppa: John Henry, from the looks of things, I'd say you're bound to be a steel-drivin' man—yup, a mighty steel-drivin' man.

Narrator 2: As John Henry's daddy spoke those words, the sky grew dark and a train whistle sounded in the distance. Then the clip-clop of hooves could be heard out on the clay road. Mama went out on the porch to have a look.

Mama: It's just a stranger dressed in black riding by on an old gray mule. . . . I don't know why, but he gives me a chill in my bones.

Narrator 1: Suddenly, John Henry's smile faded and a faraway look came into his eyes. It was almost as if he were looking into his future. What he said made his family mighty sad.

Chorus: John Henry was a little baby,
A-sittin' on his daddy's knee,
He picked up a hammer and a piece of steel,
"This hammer will be the death of me, me, me,
This hammer will be the death of me."

Narrator 2: As the months and years went by, John Henry grew stronger and stronger. By the time he was nine years old, he looked like a man even though he was still a child. He could play harder and work harder than all the other boys around. Seeing how strong John Henry was, the overseer of the plantation put him to work in the fields. There, he worked hard and bided his time. When the Civil War ended, John Henry was a full-grown man, free to seek his destiny.

Narrator 1: The United States was growing, too, stretching itself out from the Atlantic to the Pacific. In the east, in the west, and in between, settlers were clearing the land, plowing furrows, and blasting tunnels. They were building, too—homes, farms, towns, and cities. And what linked everything together? Railroads!

Chorus: Great engines went across the country,
Folks could hear their whistles blow,
The Union Pacific and the Santa Fe,
The Rock Island and the B & O, O, O,
The Rock Island and the B & O.

John Henry: That whistling is a lonesome sound, all right, but I feel like those trains are a-callin' out to me. I've got a hankering to follow them wherever they're goin'. They're tellin' me I'm meant to have a hammer in my hand. That's the only thing that'll ever ease this craving in my heart.

Poppa: You're a natural man, son, and I reckon you've gotta find your natural job.

Mama: But what about your prophecy, John Henry—that the hammer'll be the death of you?

John Henry: I've gotta do what I've gotta do, Mama. Prophecy or no prophecy, those trains are a-tellin' me I'm a hammerman.

Granddaddy: You're a fine boy, John Henry. Your blood's as red as the moon that stood still in the sky on the night you were born. And you're as strong as the river that turned 'round in its bed. I've got a feeling that you're gonna be a great man someday.

Narrator 2: So, with tears in their eyes, John Henry's family watched him walk on down the road that led to his future. John Henry traveled far and wide, doing one job and then another. At one time, he picked corn and cotton in the fields; another time, he was a roustabout for a traveling carnival; for a while, he was a deckhand on a Mississippi riverboat—the *Bayou Queen* it was called.

Narrator 1: The *Bayou Queen* carried passengers and freight to cities along the river. Whenever the riverboat docked, John Henry would load and unload the cargo. Then he'd cast off, and the *Bayou Queen* would be on its way once more.

Narrator 2: At night, when all the work was done, John Henry and his friend Joe would sit on a coil of rope under the stars and quietly sing about life on the river. One particular evening, when they were doing just that, the *Bayou Queen* suddenly lurched, groaned, and came to an abrupt halt.

John Henry: Uh-oh, feels like we're grounded!

Joe: That means trouble for sure.

John Henry: Come on, Joe, let's find out what needs doin'!

Narrator 1: The two men made their way past the frightened passengers over to where the pilot and the captain were peering over the ship's side into the muddy Mississippi.

Pilot: No question about it, sir—we've run aground on a sandbar!

Captain: Not only that, but the boat is listing! We've got to get off this sandbar or she'll capsize! There's no time to waste!

Pilot: But, Captain, we're stuck fast! There's nothing we can do!

John Henry: Begging your pardon, Cap'n, sir, but I think I can get the *Bayou Queen* off the sandbar.

Captain: John Henry, that's just bragful talk. This is no time for foolishness!

Pilot: Why not let him try, sir? We've got nothing to lose.

Captain: All right, John Henry, go ahead. But hurry!

John Henry: First thing we gotta do is to move all the stores to the stern.

Narrator 2: The crew worked feverishly hauling the cargo of barrels, bales, and crates to the rear of the ship.

Pilot: It's working, Captain. The prow has risen off the sandbar a bit.

Captain: Engage the paddle wheel! Full steam astern!

Joe: It's no good; she's still stuck fast. What'll you do now, John Henry?

John Henry: Help me, Joe. Here, tie this end of the rope to the funnel.

Narrator 1: Holding fast to the rope, John Henry lowered himself into the swirling water until he was standing on the sandbar. Then he placed his shoulder firmly against the hull of the ship.

John Henry: All right, Cap'n, try it again!

Captain: Full steam astern!

Narrator 2: The paddle wheel churned, and black smoke billowed from the funnels. As the riverboat struggled to free herself, John Henry pushed with all his strength.

Pilot: That's it—once more! We're moving! Another push and we'll be free! He's done it, Captain! We're afloat!

Joe: Here, John Henry, grab a-hold of the rope, and I'll pull you aboard!

Captain: If I hadn't seen what just happened with my own eyes, I wouldn't have believed it! I thought you were just being bragful.

John Henry: No, sir, Cap'n, sir. I'm a natural man. I say what I mean, and I mean what I say.

Narrator 1: John Henry liked working on the river. But, as always, the day came when the craving in his heart became so strong that he knew he had to move on.

John Henry: It's time for me to be leaving the river, Cap'n, sir.

Captain: I'm sorry to hear that, John Henry. Are you sure you have to go?

John Henry: Well, sir, nothing feels right in my hands—not a hoe, nor a pail, nor a rope. I guess I've gotta keep a-lookin' for my natural job, so I can work with a hammer in my hands.

Narrator 2: John Henry wandered north through Tennessee and Kentucky, looking for the kind of work that would make him happy. One day, he heard the clanging of hammers in the distance. He followed the sound until he came to the place where a crew of workers was laying the tracks for a railroad.

Narrator 1: John Henry watched them drive steel spikes into the wooden crossties that held the rails down. Three men, each with a hammer in his hand, stood around a spike. Each one, in turn, swung his hammer until they had pounded the spike into the crosstie. The falling hammers had a rhythm all their own.

Chorus: John Henry saw the hammers flying,
And he heard their silver song,
He was filled with a happiness he'd never known,
Said, "This here's the place where I belong,
    long, long,"
Said, "This here's the place where I belong."

John Henry: Mister Foreman, I'm a steel-drivin' man, and I'm looking for a job. Can you use me?

Foreman: Well, that depends on how much steel-drivin' you've done.

John Henry: I haven't done any yet, but I was born knowing how.

Foreman: That's mighty big talk, and it sounds like it's coming from a bragful man. Listen, this here's dangerous work, and if you don't know what you're doing, you could hurt somebody.

John Henry: Nobody will get hurt, mister, 'cause I can drive that there spike all by myself. If you just give me a

hammer and somebody holds the spike for me, I'll show you.

Foreman: Well, that beats all! Who in their right mind would hold a spike for a man who's never driven steel before?

Li'l Bill: I'll hold it for him, boss.

Foreman: You trying to get yourself killed, Li'l Bill?

Narrator 2: Li'l Bill answered by kneeling down and setting a spike on a crosstie. Then he motioned to John Henry.

Li'l Bill: Go ahead, mister. Pick out one of those hammers on the ground over there.

John Henry: I'll take this one.

Li'l Bill: You sure? That's a mighty heavy one—a twelve-pounder.

John Henry: I'm sure. It feels right natural in my hands.

Narrator 1: All the men looked at each other knowingly, as if to say, "We never did hear such big talk in all our born days!" Then they watched as John Henry stepped up to the spike.

Li'l Bill: You've gotta tap it down gentle-like the first time around.

Narrator 2: But John Henry was already bringing that hammer down with all his might. It rang out like silver as he hit the spike right on the head. Then, before anyone could say a word, he swung again, and this time the hammer rang out like gold as he buried the spike in the crosstie.

Foreman: Son, you're hired!

Li'l Bill: And I'll hold the spikes for you. Yessir, I'll be your shaker.

Foreman: Well, John Henry, I thought you were being bragful, but I see that you can do what you said you would.

John Henry: Mister Foreman, I say what I mean, and I mean what I say. And like I said, I'm a natural steel-drivin' man.

Narrator 1: So that's the way John Henry became a steel-driver. Li'l Bill worked as his shaker—setting the spike for John Henry to hit, then shaking it and turning it for the next blow of the hammer. John Henry could drive a spike in from any direction—up, down, or sideways, it was all the same to him. He never missed, and he never got tired.

Chorus: Each morning, as the sun was rising,
And the birds began to sing,
All the folks for a mile or more would greet the day,
A-hearing John Henry's hammers ring, ring, ring,
A-hearing John Henry's hammers ring.

Narrator 2: The more John Henry drove that steel, the faster and stronger he became.

John Henry: Li'l Bill, this twelve-pound hammer is too light for me. It's slowin' me down.

Li'l Bill: Why don't you try a twenty-pounder, John Henry?

John Henry: Why, thank you, Li'l Bill. That's a good idea. I'll try two twenty-pounders—one in each hand.

Narrator 1: One day, the story goes, the crew had almost finished laying down the track.

Foreman: Just a hundred yards left, and we can call it a day. . . . Hey, what's that I see moving up the line?

Workman 1: It's the 5:15 express, and it's coming right at us—at fifty miles an hour!

Foreman: But the signal flag is up! How come the engineer's not stopping?

Workman 2: I reckon the sun's in his eyes, and he can't see the flag!

Foreman: What'll we do? It won't take but a few minutes for that train to reach the end of this track. We're gonna have us a terrible wreck!

John Henry: You men there, get back out of the way! Hurry!

Narrator 2: John Henry coiled up the remaining hundred yards of steel track and hung it on his shoulder just like it was a rope. He grabbed one end and swung it over his head, and then he let it go. It flew out straight, and it fell into its proper place on the crossties.

Li'l Bill: Hurry, John Henry. That train's a-comin' lickety-split!

Chorus: John Henry grabbed his twenty-pounder,
Didn't hesitate, not at all,
He ran down the track as fast as he could go,
Yessir, how he made those hammers fall, fall, fall,
Yessir, how he made those hammers fall.

Workman 1: How that man can go! Look at him! He spits out those spikes between his teeth and pounds them right into place. I think he's gonna beat the train, yes sirree, I really do!

Narrator 1: John Henry pounded in the last spike and jumped aside just as the 5:15 roared past him.

Foreman: There's not another man alive who could have saved that train, John Henry. The engineer didn't even know what danger he was in. You're a hero!

Narrator 2: After that incident, John Henry's fame spread far and wide. People came from the north, east, south, and west to watch him drive steel. Sometimes a girl named Polly Ann was in the crowd. John Henry sure was happy on those days. And he was happiest on the day that he and Polly Ann were married.

Polly Ann often came to watch her husband work and to join in the songs that he and Li'l Bill sang to the clang of the hammers. One time, she did much more than just sing.

Chorus: John Henry had a little woman,
And her name was Polly Ann,
When John Henry was sick and lying in his bed,
She drove in those spikes like any man, man, man,
She drove in those spikes like any man.

Narrator 1: On another day, when Polly Ann arrived at the railhead, she found the air crackling with excitement.

Polly Ann: Lands sake! Why, you're all fired up like a locomotive. What's happening, John Henry?

John Henry: The Chesapeake and Ohio Railroad sent the word out—they're gonna be blasting a tunnel through a mountain in Summers County, West Virginia.

Polly Ann: Sounds like mighty hard work, blasting through a mountain of stone.

Li'l Bill: That's for sure! That's why they're paying twice as much as anyone else.

Workman 2: Yeah, twice the pay for ten times the work and a hundred times the danger!

Workman 1: The C & O wants the best hammermen there are.

Polly Ann: Well, John Henry, if they want the best, then they're going to be a-needin' you.

John Henry: And Li'l Bill, too. I'm not gonna go without him.

Li'l Bill: All right, I'm willin', John Henry. Do you see that stranger dressed in black moving on down the road on his old gray mule? We can follow right behind him.

John Henry: All right, then. . . .Why don't you two start, and I'll catch up with you.

Polly Ann: What's the matter, John Henry? Looks like a cloud's come over you. Are you ailing?

John Henry: Seems like all of a sudden the day's turned sad, and I'm feelin' a chill in my bones.

Li'l Bill: That's just cause a big black thunderhead's come along and covered up the sun.

John Henry: Maybe so. Pay it no mind, Polly Ann. A man's gotta do what a man's gotta do. Come on, we're on our way.

Narrator 2: So John Henry, Polly Ann, and Li'l Bill went to Summers County in West Virginia, where the Big Bend Tunnel was to be built through a mountain of solid rock. Cap'n Tommy, the tunnel foreman, was surrounded by hundreds of men looking for jobs as hammermen, shakers, blacksmiths, and water carriers. But after studying the site, many thought that the mountain was too powerful, and the job too risky.

Workman 3: 'Tain't no use. This old mountain's been a-sittin' here a mighty long time. No way it's gonna let us tunnel through it a mile or more.

Workman 1: You're right, it can't be done. There's no point tryin' to drive steel through all this rock.

John Henry: Who says so? I'm a natural steel-drivin' man, and I'm aiming to make a hole through this mountain from one side to the other. Let's get started, Li'l Bill. Hold one of those drills up against that mountain face!

Narrator 1: Li'l Bill did. Using a seventy-pound hammer, John Henry whacked that long, sharp steel drill and cracked part of the rock face with one great blow. Then he used his twenty-pounders to drive the drill farther and farther in. Between blows, Li'l Bill shook the drill so that the rock dust would

fall away. After John Henry made the hole deep enough, the blasting crew filled it with dynamite and blew the rock apart. As John Henry's drills got dull, the blacksmiths sharpened them in the fire.

Cap'n Tommy: Well, if that don't beat all! I never saw a man dull so many drills in one day. I need a crew of blacksmiths just for you, John Henry! You can do the work of ten men, sure enough, just like you said.

John Henry: Yessir, Cap'n Tommy, I'm a natural man—I say what I mean, and I mean what I say.

Narrator 2: As time went on, many of the men took sick from the smoke of the lamps and the dust of the shale—tunnel sickness it was called. Lives were taken by falling rocks, too.

Narrator 1: Despite all the hardships and the hazards, the work went forward—day after day, week after week, month after month. The songs the workers sang helped keep the rhythm of the hammers.

Chorus: John Henry said to his shaker,
"Oh, shaker, why don't you sing?
For I'm swinging twenty pounds from my arms
    on down,
Just listen to that cold steel ring, ring, ring,
Just listen to that cold steel ring."

Narrator 2: John Henry had never been so happy. Then one day, a fast-talking, tongue-wagging salesman approached Cap'n Tommy.

Salesman: Howdy, Cap'n Tommy. I've got a newfangled, new-fashioned, up-to-the-minute, brand new machine here that can out-drive, out-work, out-drill, and out-last your five fastest men put together. It's called a steam drill. It works on steam power, not man power, so it never gets tired and it never needs sleep.

Cap'n Tommy: I reckon I don't need any machine. I've got the best steel-drivin' man in the world working for me. His name is John Henry. Why, he can drill holes faster than ten men working together!

Salesman: That so?

Cap'n Tommy: It sure is. Why, John Henry's so fast, we've got to pour buckets of ice water on the handles of his hammers to keep 'em from catching fire.

Salesman: Of course, I've heard of John Henry. But after all, sir, a man is nothing but a man. I assure you, Cap'n Tommy, there's not a man alive who can drill faster than my honest-to-goodness guaranteed, warranteed, one-hundred-percent nickel-plated steam drill.

Cap'n Tommy: You're wasting your time, sir, and mine, too.

Salesman: Let's not be hasty, Cap'n. I wouldn't want you to regret your decision. You know the old saying, "Act in haste, repent at leisure."

Cap'n Tommy: See here, sir!

Salesman: Tell you what I'm going to do, Cap'n. To show you how confident I am of my machine, I'm willing to have a contest between your man and my steam drill. If your man wins, you get to keep the drill absolutely free and clear, no charge, gratis, no strings attached! If your man loses, you buy my steam drill. What do you say?

Cap'n Tommy: Well . . . that sounds fair enough. But I'll have to talk it over with John Henry before deciding.

Salesman: Go right ahead, sir. I'd be happy to come back tomorrow.

Narrator 1: Cap'n Tommy told John Henry what the salesman had said.

Cap'n Tommy: What do you think, son?

John Henry: Cap'n, a machine ain't nothin' but a machine. I'm a natural steel-drivin' man, and I don't want any machine taking away the happiest work I ever had. Course I'll race that steam drill, and I'll beat it, too!

Chorus: John Henry said to Cap'n Tommy,
"A man ain't nothin' but a man,
And before I would let that steam drill beat me down,
I'd die with this hammer in my hand, hand, hand,
I'd die with this hammer in my hand."

Narrator 2: So, the contest was agreed upon. When word got out that John Henry was racing a newfangled machine, the excitement quickly spread across the countryside. Folks came from Pennsylvania, Virginia, and Kentucky just to watch. The first thing they saw was the gleaming steam drill with its twenty-foot steam boiler and its crew of operators. Soon the contest judge began to get things organized.

Judge: Mister Salesman, have your crew set that steam drill over there to the left of the tunnel so everyone can see.

Salesman: All right now, easy does it! I don't want any dents, nicks, bumps, or scratches! Better give it a few extra squirts of grease and oil, and be sure you've got a good fire going under that boiler. This is going to be a rip-roaring, foot-stomping, flag-waving race, and I aim to win!

Judge: And you, John Henry, you're over here to the right of the tunnel.

Cap'n Tommy: How're you doing, John Henry? We've got a pile of sharpened drills all ready for you, and Li'l Bill's got a bucket of ice water. You all set?

John Henry: I sure am, Cap'n. I've got my brand new thirty-pound hammer—I call it Polly Ann just for luck. I'm a-raring to go.

Judge: Are you ready? When you see me drop my hat, that's the signal for the race to begin.

Cap'n Tommy: Good luck, John Henry!

Narrator 1: The judge gave the signal. John Henry swung his hammer, and it rang out silver against the drill that Li'l Bill was holding up against the mountain. The steam drill hissed and puffed as its drill bit into the stone. Everyone's eyes slid back and forth from one to the other. It was a full hour before anyone even spoke.

John Henry: How we doing, Li'l Bill?

Li'l Bill: The machine's ahead, John Henry.

John Henry: Don't you fret; just keep shaking that drill. And give me another thirty-pounder—that's what I need, a hammer in each hand. I'm just warmin' up!

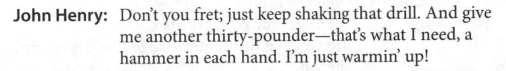

Workman 3: Look at those hammers fly! Why, they're glowing like coals. John Henry's catching up!

Workman 2: Yup, he might even win!

Salesman: John Henry beat my steam drill? No sirree, never! Not till fish fly, ducks dance, and cows crow! Stoke up that boiler, boys! More steam is what we need! That's it! That should do it!

Narrator 2: But as the steam drill speeded up, so did John Henry. He hammered so fast and so hard, the nails in his shoes started to shake.

Cap'n Tommy: It's been four hours since the race started, John Henry. How're you feelin'?

John Henry: I'm feelin' like I just got outta bed, Cap'n. How's that machine feelin'?

Cap'n Tommy: The drill got busted, so they had to stop and fix it. You're going to pull ahead!

Chorus: John Henry shouted to the salesman,
"That steam drill's givin' you a sign,

When the rocks in these mountains turn to
  precious gold,
Your steam drill might beat these arms of mine,
  mine, mine,
Your steam drill might beat these arms of mine."

Narrator 1: After a bit, the steam drill started up again a-clanging and a-hissing away, but John Henry made an extra effort, too. Five hours went by, then six, then seven. Sweat poured down John Henry's back, but he kept his hammer ringing out loud and clear. Li'l Bill kept shaking the drills, and Polly Ann kept giving him water and singing him songs.

Chorus: Oh, Polly brought a little water,
Then she brought a little tea,
She sang out her hammer songs the whole day long,
She sang just as sweetly as could be, be, be,
She sang just as sweetly as could be.

John Henry: How we doing now, Li'l Bill?

Li'l Bill: You're ahead, John Henry! There's only one hour left. I reckon you're going to win, if you can keep a-goin'!

John Henry: I'm weary, but I won't stop. I'll drop with my hammer in my hands before I let that machine beat me!

Workman 2: I don't see how John Henry can keep going.

Workman 1: I don't see how the machine can keep going.

Workman 3: They don't have much time left. This here contest is supposed to be nine hours long, and it's almost that now.

Narrator 2: At the end of the ninth hour, precisely, the judge dropped his hat once more.

Polly Ann: The race is over, John Henry! The judge is coming over to measure!

Narrator 1: As the judge compared how deep the man and the machine had drilled, John Henry leaned wearily against the mountain. There wasn't a single sound to be heard; all eyes were riveted on the judge. Finally, he whispered something in Cap'n Tommy's ear, after which Cap'n Tommy pointed to the salesman and addressed the crowd.

Chorus: "You see what happened, Mister Salesman,
You thought you were mighty fine,
But John Henry, he drove those drills in
    fourteen feet,
The steam drill, it only drove them nine, nine, nine,
The steam drill, it only drove them nine!"

All: [sounds of cheering]

Polly Ann: You did it, John Henry! You won!

John Henry: That I did, Polly Ann. I beat that machine just like I said I would, 'cause I'm a natural steel-drivin' man.

Cap'n Tommy: I'm mighty proud of you, John Henry.

John Henry: It takes muscle to drive steel; muscle, not steam.

Narrator 2: Then, suddenly, the words died on John Henry's lips; the smile left his face, and the sparkle went out of his eye. He slumped to the ground. Polly Ann knelt down and cradled his head in her lap.

Polly Ann: What's the matter, John Henry? Are you ailing?

John Henry: I feel like I'm dying, Polly Ann.

Polly Ann: Cap'n Tommy! Get a doctor!

John Henry: No use. I say what I mean, and I mean what I say. I'm done.

Narrator 1: And with that, John Henry laid down his hammer and closed his eyes forever. Just then, the clip-clop of hooves could be heard in the distance. As the crowd watched silently, a stranger dressed in

black on an old gray mule paused to observe the scene. Then slowly, with bowed head, the stranger resumed his slow pace down the dusty road.

Chorus: Oh, here's what happened to John Henry,
Who battered that mountainside,
He hammered so hard, he broke his poor old heart,
He laid down his hammer and he died, died, died,
He laid down his hammer and he died.
They took John Henry to the graveyard,
They buried him in the sand,
And every great engine that goes a-roaring by,
Whistles, "There lies a steel-drivin' man, man, man,"
Whistles, "There lies a steel-drivin' man."

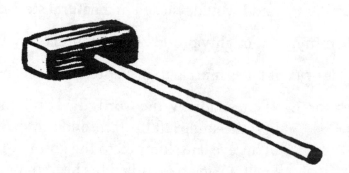

Think-Aloud
COPYING MASTERS

I wonder . . .

Think-Aloud Copying Master 1

I made a connection when . . .

Think-Aloud Copying Master 2   251

I was able
to picture
in my mind . . .

I figured out _____ because . . .

I noticed the author used . . .

Think-Aloud Copying Master 5

I thought _____ was important in this text because . . .

Think-Aloud Copying Master 6 255

Think-Aloud Copying Master 7

When I read _____,
I had to re-read,
read back, read on . . .

LITERATURE INDEX by GENRE

Biography and Autobiography

Fiction

Dramatic Monologue

Realistic Fiction

Folk Tales, Tall Tales, and Fables

Nonfiction

Articles

Informational Nonfiction

ACKNOWLEDGMENTS

continued from page 2

"Sea Talk" by Max Fatchen from ANOTHER FOURTH POETRY BOOK compiled by John Foster. Copyright © 1989 by John Foster. Used by permission of Oxford University Press.

"Better Than Gold" by Maria Testa from *Child Life*, May/June 2003. Copyright © 2003 by Children's Better Health Institute, Benjamin Franklin Literary & Medical Society, Inc. Used by permission of Children's Better Health Institute, Benjamin Franklin Literary & Medical Society, Inc.

"The Riding Machine" by Barbara Hagen from *Boys' Quest*; Oct./Nov. 2003, Vol. 9, Issue 3. Copyright © 2003 by Bluffton News Publishing. Used by permission of Bluffton News Publishing.

"The Sayings of Confucius" from SOURCES OF CHINESE TRADITION, edited by William Theodore de Bary. Copyright © 1965 by Columbia University Press.

"Jump Start: An After-School Program Kids Leap At" by Scott Ingram from *Current Health*, September 2004. Copyright © 2004 by Weekly Reader Corporation. Used by permission of Weekly Reader Corporation.

"Clever Manka" by Parker Fillmore from THE SHEPHERD'S NOSEGAY: STORIES FROM FINLAND AND CZECHOSLOVAKIA. Copyright © 1958 by Parker Fillmore. Used by permission of Harcourt Brace Inc.

Excerpt from ULTIMATE KIDS' MONEY BOOK by Neale S. Godfrey. Copyright © 1998 by Children's Financial Network, Inc. Used by permission of Simon & Schuster Books for Young Readers.

"Rock Hound" by Kristin Baird Rattini from *Boys' Life*, December 2002. Copyright © 2002 by the Boy Scouts of America. Used by permission of the Boy Scouts of America.

"Words Do Not Pay" by Chief Joseph from IN A SACRED MANNER I LIVE: NATIVE AMERICAN WISDOM edited by Neil Philip. Copyright © 1997 by The Albion Press Ltd. Used by permission of Clarion Books, a Houghton Mifflin Company imprint.

"At the Medici Villa" by the Virtual Renaissance Team. Copyright © ___ by ___. Used by permission of ___.

"There was a young lady named Bright" by A. H. Reginald Butler, and "A scientist living at Staines" by R. J. P. Hewison. Originally appeared in *Punch*. Copyright © Punch/Rothco.

"A luckless time-traveler from Lynn," from GHASTLIES, GOOPS & PINCUSHIONS by X. J. Kennedy. Copyright © 1989 by X. J. Kennedy. Reprinted with permission of Margaret K. McElderry Books, an imprint of Simon & Schuster Children's Publishing Division.

"The Touch of Sense" by John Kitching from ANOTHER FOURTH POETRY BOOK compiled by John Foster. Copyright © 1989 by John Foster. Used by permission of Oxford University Press.

Excerpt ("The People, Who Were They?") from STORIES ON STONE: ROCK ART: IMAGES FROM THE ANCIENT ONES by Jennifer Owings Dewey. Copyright © 1996 by Jennifer Owings Dewey. Used by permission of Little Brown and Company.

"Volcano!" by Stephen James O'Meara from *Odyssey Magazine*. Copyright © ___ by Gallaudet University. Used by permission of Gallaudet University.

"Volcano!" by Stephen James O'Meara from Odyssey Magazine. Copyright © ___ by Gallaudet University. Used by permission of Gallaudet University.

Cover Illustration: Amanda Hall

Illustration Credits: Marika Hann, 9–13; David Erickson, 14–18, 92–95; Karen Stormer Brooks, 19–22; Sandy Rabinowitz, 23–26; Barbara Pollack, 27–30, 45–53; Kate Flanagan, 31–33, 166–175; Dorothy Reinhardt, 34–39; Betsy James, 40–44, 150–165; Stephen Marchesi, 54–57; Joel Iskowitz, 58–61; Janet Montecalvo, 62–64; Gerry O'Neill, 65–67; Tatjana Mai–Wyss, 68–72; Gil Ashby, 73–75; Hugh Harrison, 76–79; Kelly Murphy, 80–82; Susan Spellman, 83–87, 176–199; Dan Krovatin, 88–91, 226–248; Gershom Griffith, 96–100; Kathleen Kemly, 101–107, 200–225; Pam Carroll, 108–112, 142–149; Timothy Otis, 113–117; Roman Dunets, 118–120; Valerie Sokolova, 121–125; Donald Cook, 126–128; Laurie Harden, 129–131; Janet Hamlin, 132–135; Ka Botzis, 136–139